Simon Henry

The Party Dress

How to make the perfect one for you

GUILD OF MASTER
CRAFTSMAN PUBLICATIONS

First published 2009 by

GUILD OF MASTER CRAFTSMAN PUBLICATIONS LTD

166 High Street, Lewes, East Sussex, BN7 1XU

Text © Simon Henry 2009
© Copyright in the Work, Guild of Master Craftsman Publications Ltd, 2009

ISBN 978-1-86108-666-2

A catalogue record of this book is available from the British Library.

Associate Publisher **JONATHAN BAILEY**
Production Manager **JIM BULLEY**
Managing Editor **GERRIE PURCELL**
Senior Project Editor **VIRGINIA BREHAUT**
Copy Editor **ALISON HOWARD**
Managing Art Editor **GILDA PACITTI**
Photographer **CHRIS GLOAG**
Stylist **LOUISE COMPAGNONE**

Colour origination **GMC REPROGRAPHICS**
Printed and bound by **HING YIP PRINTING CO. LTD.**

For Clive and Mum who
tell me often that they
are proud of me, and for
Veronica, Dad and Hazel:
I think that if they were
still with us they
would be proud.

I HAVE ALWAYS BELIEVED IN THEATRE, FANTASY and the importance of making an impact. Party dresses and evening gowns are the perfect must-have garments to ensure that you will be the belle of the ball.

I have dressed many celebrities for weddings, black tie events and awards ceremonies and they all have the same wish...'to make an entrance, look super-sophisticated and turn heads'.

Special occasions require special dresses! The party dress makes a shrine of your wardrobe – it is a garment that will hold everlasting memories from that special evening.

Throughout time, couture gowns have inspired designers, stylists and models all over the world and continue to do so today.

Enjoy making and wearing your own special gown.

Ian Stuart

Award-winning Designer of Couture Gowns

Contents

1
Getting Started

2
Making the Blocks

3
The Dresses

Putting on the Ritz

Making yourself the gown or party dress of your dreams may sound daunting, but I assure you that, even if you have never sewn a stitch before, you can do it. From flowing, draped styles to boned, corseted bodices, read on and I will show you how...

How many times in your life do you get to wear a gown or a sparkly party dress? If you are like most girls, the first 'formal' you attend will be your school prom. Later, if you are lucky, you may be invited to the occasional ball or premiere, followed by what is probably the most special of events, your wedding.

Gowns and party dresses can be very expensive. If you decide to buy 'off the peg', you will find that manufacturers make hundreds, if not thousands, of dresses in the same style, and mostly, they will not even fit you properly. This

means you are quite likely to attend a function and find someone else wearing exactly the same dress – and it probably won't fit them either!

This book is intended for people with little or no sewing experience, so there are some shortcuts and cheats. Some fellow designers have looked at this course and thrown up their hands in horror at some of the things I will tell you to do. But remember, this is your dress; I am not teaching you to do this for a living. My respectful answer to those critics is just this: it works!

The Prom dress

'Prom' is short for 'promenade' and derives from the time when debutantes were presented at Court. A *débutante*, from the French meaning 'female beginner', was a young lady from an upper-class family who had reached the age of maturity, and was ready for her formal introduction into society. When she was presented at Court, part of the purpose was to display her to eligible bachelors. She would be dressed in the very best gown her family could afford and walked or 'promenaded' at a formal ball so that all could see her. It would then be said that she had made her debut.

Nowadays, a prom ball is often held at the end of schooling, but a young lady may still be said to have made her debut. I love the idea of girls attending their first formal event, the school prom. Imagine what a thrill it will be to dress up like a princess and, for the first time, have all attention focused on you. But prom time is difficult for parents, who worry 'who will ask her?'; 'will he be suitable?'; 'what is she going to wear?' and 'how will we afford it?'

Most girls would be horrified by the idea of their parents helping them to make their prom dress, but if you think about it, most of your friends will be going to the same shops. It is quite likely that one, two or more of them will turn up in the same dress. But if you design and make your own, you will be the only girl in the whole world to wear that dress!

Planning your ball or 'red carpet' gown

If your gown is for a ball or a special event like a premiere or an opening, consider your style carefully. Will your gown travel well? Will it photograph well? Will you have to sit in it for long periods of time?

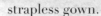

Look at fashion magazines and try to find a style that will suit your figure; one that will produce the 'wow' factor yet still be appropriate for your age. Try not to go for boring black: pick something that will stand out in a crowd. Don't go for white or pastel shades unless they are perfect for your colouring because they can make you look as though you have just come from a wedding. Be bold, and have fun!

Remember your age: you don't want to look as though you have just disembarked from *The Good Ship Lollipop*, but you don't want to look as if you work in a lap-dancing club either. You may want to look sexy, but trust me: allure is far more about what you don't show than what you do.

I made one of the worst mistakes of my design career by dressing a local dignitary for a film premiere in a very tight, strapless gown.

She was so uncomfortable that she asked her escort to undo the back of the dress while they were watching the film – and I bet you know what's coming! When the film ended she stood up, forgetting that the gown was undone. Before she realised her mistake, and in front of the assembled press and members of the public, it slid elegantly to the floor. Fortunately, she was wearing very nice foundation garments, and her escort was very quick to drape his coat over her so she could maintain as much dignity as possible under the circumstances.

I am very lucky that the lady in question is still a very good client of mine, and, while we laugh about the incident now, it would never have happened if I had thought about the purpose of the gown as well as the look of it. I urge you to do the same!

How to Use this Book

This book is structured very simply. Start at the beginning and work your way through. Read the whole thing first so you know what's coming next: that way there won't be any nasty surprises.

Instead of purchased patterns we're going to use very old couture methods to create a dress that fits you perfectly, made from your own pattern or 'body block'. Every time you read the word 'block', imagine it as your 'personal pattern'.

Look on this book as a course, with each section or exercise as a precursor to the next. Follow the sections systematically, sewing each exercise as you go, not moving on to the next until you're confident with each one. Read the instructions very carefully, even if you can sew don't assume that I'll be using the techniques you're accustomed to.

My method is one that I have designed and used over many years. It has been tested on a number of students, some with lots of experience and others with very little. It has been further refined so that it can be used by almost anyone. Only the other day, I asked my partner to insert an invisible zip as a way of testing out the teaching techniques. Although he hadn't used a sewing machine before, claiming that he couldn't even sew on a button, he did it perfectly on the third attempt! Now he wants to finish the entire sewing course. I've created a monster!

Don't try out these exercises alone; you will need help making your body block as well as with the fittings. I suggest that you approach the projects as a team effort. Get yourself a sewing partner.

You don't have to be an experienced machinist to use this book, although it will obviously take you longer if you haven't sewn before. But if you or a sewing partner can sew a straight line, you'll be fine.

I like the idea of groups of you getting together for fitting evenings or 'gin and pin' parties. Make an event out of it, arrange to meet regularly to help each other with fittings and so on. Perhaps one of you will find the whole process easier than others and can help the group through difficulties. Try it, mix a pitcher of martini and see how you get on.

Getting Started

'The difference between style and fashion is quality.'

GIORGIO ARMANI

Equipment and Materials

Gather all of your equipment together before you start so you can get on with the job without stopping to look for missing items. Clear a space for yourself, lock out the children and the cat, and let's make a start.

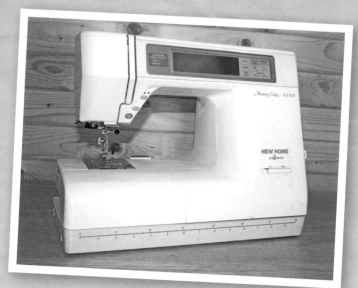

Sewing machine

As long as your machine sews both straight stitch and zigzag, you will be able to follow the methods in this book.

Over the years, I have upgraded to the most advanced machines, spending thousands of pounds on the latest computer embroidery technology. To be honest, though, most of the time I only use the straight and zigzag stitches. If you don't have a machine yet, get hold of a basic one. Your local supplier will recommend something suitable, either new or used.

Auction websites are also good for second-hand machines. But, if you go down this road, be sure to have it professionally serviced so that it runs smoothly and the tension is set. Buy new needles to suit individual fabrics.

Whatever you do, don't be tempted to buy an industrial machine just yet. They run too fast and you don't have the same control as a domestic one. If your machine has an adjustable speed, start with it on slow or medium until you are confident that you can control a straight stitching line – then you can gradually begin to increase speed.

Take long strips of your waste fabric and practise sewing seams with a ⅝ inch (1.5cm) seam allowance. Press the seam open and check that there is no pulling or puckering. If there is, adjust the tension setting on your machine to compensate. Refer to the operating manual for individual machines as they will all vary slightly.

Overlocker or serger

An overlocker is very useful for finishing off seams and neatening hems, but is by no means an essential piece of equipment. You can finish seams very well by using the zigzag setting on your normal machine. If you are lucky enough to have access to an overlocker, practise stitching long strips of waste fabric before pressing with a steam iron. Check that the seam is not gathered or stretched. If so, adjust the tension according to the manufacturer's instructions.

The dress stand

A dress stand or tailor's dummy isn't really necessary for this project but is helpful for doing your own fittings. A professional stand can cost a great deal of money and isn't even adjustable. You should be able to pick up a home-use, adjustable one for a very reasonable price – there are plenty available on internet auction sites – then you'll have it for future projects.

I use a professional one (affectionately known as Dolly), which will be used for demonstrating exercises throughout this book. As I can draw and pin directly on to 'her', it will be easier for you to understand the principles – and I don't think a live model would take very kindly to such treatment. You will also be able to better imagine the dresses on yourself if we don't use a live model.

Dress stand

are also helpful. They are not expensive, and prevent sticking with even the most delicate fabrics.

You also need a sturdy ironing board with a clean cover. I buy a new cover for each dress I make, but this is probably a bit extreme. At the very least, buy a white or natural cover as coloured ones can bleed onto your fabrics. A sleeve board, a small ironing board for pressing sleeves which fits onto your table or board, is also useful for pressing darts open as well as for getting into tight corners.

Always do a test strip for each new fabric to get the settings on your iron just right. You want the iron and steam to be just hot enough to press the seams flat, but not so hot that the fabric shrinks.

Your iron

The importance of having a good iron cannot be stressed enough. Many a good gown has been ruined when my iron discharges its scaly contents all over lovely, pristine silk.

Whereas professional steam-generated irons were very expensive in the past, they are becoming increasingly affordable. I recently saw one on a home shopping channel for a very reasonable price. A steam generator iron makes the steam in a separate tank so it is very 'dry', cutting down the chance of wetting your fabrics. Iron shields, made from heat-resistant plastic that fits on the sole plate of your iron,

Scissors

Every budding seamstress needs a good pair of scissors or tailoring shears. Make sure they are sharp and you only use them on fabric. Buy the best ones you can afford so they last for years. Mine were purchased over 15 years ago and they are still going strong!

Scissors

Calico (unbleached muslin or quilter's cotton)

Metre rule

Here is a list of other pieces of equipment you will need (you may have most of these already):

- Pins
- Marker pens
- Metre rule or long straight edge
- Designer's square – used as a set square and for adding seam allowances
- Tailor's chalk
- Tape measure
- Rouleau hook (this will be explained later – see page 47)
- Sketchpad and pencils
- Seam ripper
- Small fabric snips
- Spirit level (not essential, but can be handy if you don't have a good eye for lining up straight edges)
- Pattern paper or large sheets of brown paper

Fabrics

You will also need a good supply of medium-weight calico (known as unbleached muslin or quilter's cotton in the U.S.). This will be used for our practice exercises: to make a body block (a pattern moulded to your body) and a toile (a mock-up of the actual dress that will be unpicked later to form the pattern for the final dress). Buy about 11 yards (10 metres) or so. It is fairly inexpensive and it's best to make mistakes at this price.

Seam ripper

Tailor's chalk

Rouleau hook

Tape measure

Pins

Fabric snips

Sewing Techniques

This section features simple sewing techniques that are not only essential for making your party dress, but are fundamental to nearly all sewing projects you encounter. Get them right now, and everything else later will seem easy.

Sewing a Straight Seam

This is not as straightforward as it sounds. There are several things to consider before you even touch your sewing machine.

Consider the type of fabric you are using. Thicker fabrics such as calico need a tension setting and needle size different from those used for very fine silk. Refer to the instructions that came with your machine, which will explain the different tension, pressure and needles used for different fabric weights. Every manufacturer and machine uses slightly different settings.

Make sure you use the right thread type for individual fabrics. A general, multi-purpose thread will be fine for your practice pieces, body block and toile; but you need specific thread types for different weights of fabric.

Do a test run on long strips of waste fabric or calico. This is not only good practice, but tests whether your machine tension is set up correctly.

Let's start to sew!

1 The recommended seam allowance throughout this book is ⅝ inch (1.5cm). Seam allowance is the distance that we sew in from the side edge of the garment pieces. There will be markings on the plate of your machine but, to make it easier to begin with, stick a piece of coloured tape to the base plate ⅝ inch (1.5cm) from the needle. We will call this the marker.

2 Position your fabric strips with the 'right sides' together and the edges lined up. The 'right side' of the fabric is the side that faces out on your finished garment. With patterned fabrics, for example, this will be the clear, brightly coloured side.

1

2

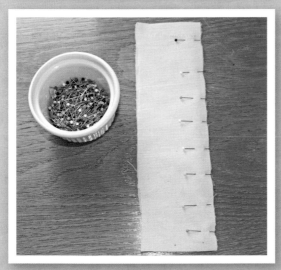

3

4

3 Pin the strips together at right angles to the stitching line about every 2 inches (5cm) or so. You can sew quite happily along the stitching line without removing the pins. This speeds up stitching as it eliminates the need for tacking.

4 Place the pinned strips under the needle, lining the edge up with the marker.

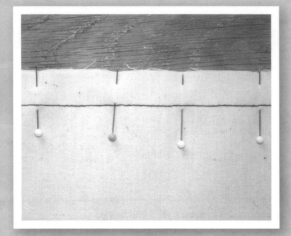

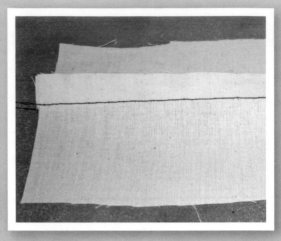

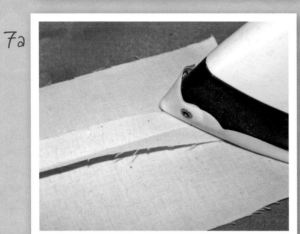

7a

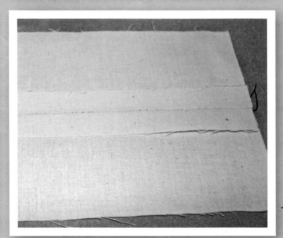

7b

5 Start stitching slowly, going forwards by two or three stitches, then push the reverse button and sew the same backwards. This will make a 'lock stitch' so that the seam does not come undone.

6 Now slowly stitch a straight line, keeping the edges of the fabric running along the marker so that you are stitching ⅝ inch (1.5cm) in from the edge. When you get to the end of the seam, sew back two or three stitches and forward two or three stitches, just as at the beginning of the seam. This will lock off the end of the seam.

7 Open up the seam allowance and press flat (**7a**). Now, stand back and admire your own work (**7b**). Well done you!

Do a few more strips in the same way. It is a good idea to speed up a little each time until you are confident that you can sew an accurate, straight seam.

Sewing Around Curves

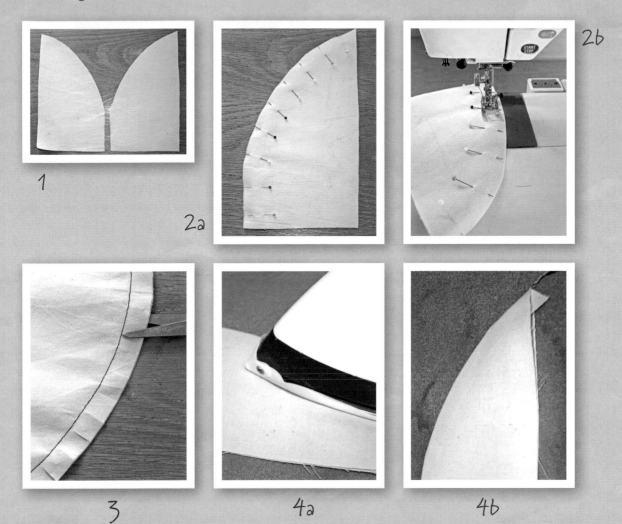

1

2a

2b

3

4a

4b

Two curves facing the same way

These can be sewn in just the same way as straight seams, keeping the edge of the fabric against the marker as you move carefully around.

1 To practise this method, cut out two identical pieces of calico: right angles joined by a curve.

2 Pin together (**2a**), and then sew (**2b**).

3 Using sharp scissors, snip into the seam allowance, every 2 inches (5cm) or so, to within ⅟₁₆ inch (2mm) of the stitching line. This is called 'notching', and will be referred to throughout the book.

4 Turn right sides out and press (**4a**). The seam should be smooth, with no sharp angles (**4b**).

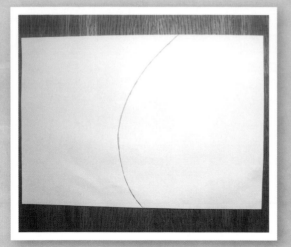

1

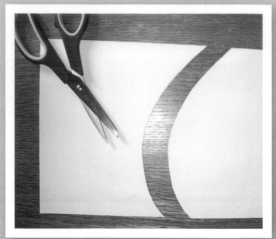

2a

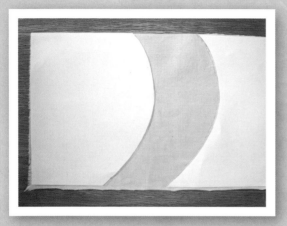

2b

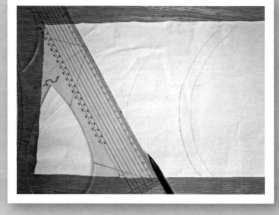

3a

One curve in and one curve out

You may want to sew a curved seam into a flat piece of fabric, such as sewing a skirt onto a curved bodice seam.

It is important to note that the stitching line should be ⅝ inch (1.5cm) in from the edge of your fabric. This is the line that you have to match when sewing the two pieces together, rather than the edge of the fabric.

Let me show you.

1 Begin by drawing a gentle curve on a piece of paper.

2 Cut along the line (**2a**) and lay it out on your piece of calico; trace around the pattern (**2b**) and mark the fabric.

3 Using the designer's set square, add a seam allowance of ⅝ inch (1.5cm) to the curved edges (**3a**).

The Party Dress

3b

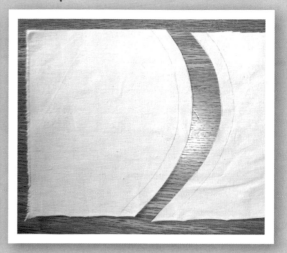

4

5a

5b

6

4 Cut out the pattern pieces.

5 Notch (snip into) the edge of the pieces on the stitching line, then fold in half and notch the centre line in the seam allowance on both (**5a & 5b**).

6 With the right sides together, match up the notches and pin at right angles to the seam line.

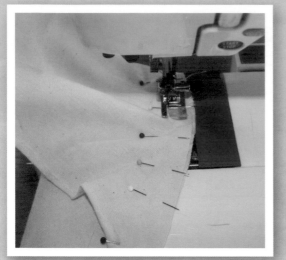

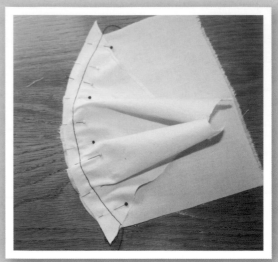

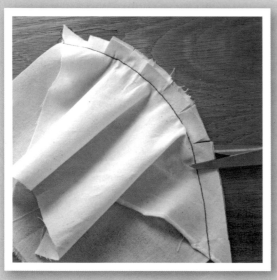

8

9

7 Now stitch with your machine, keeping the edge of your fabric along the marker; ease the fabric together as you go (**7a & 7b**).

8 Snip into the seam allowance, almost down to the stitching line as we did before, about 2 inches (5cm) apart.

9 Open out the curved pieces and smooth them out with your hand.

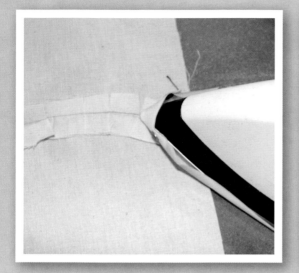

11

10 Press the seam open so that the fabric lies flat with a curved seam (**10a & 10b**).

11 Now turn over to the 'right side' of the fabric and sing yourself praise.

Repeat a few more times, using curves of different sizes, until you feel confident and understand the principle of the technique.

Once you have mastered straight and curved seams, you can pretty much sew anything. It's only a matter of practice and confidence. All of the seams described in this book will be straight, curved or a combination of both.

Darts

Darts are a way of reducing or suppressing fabric when you don't want to shape a garment using full seams. They can be either straight or curved. The classic use of darts is at the waist-to-hip suppression on skirts and trousers or the waist-to-bust, bust-to-shoulder, or hip-to-waist-to-bust-to-shoulder suppression on dresses. Some darts, like waist-to-hip or shoulder-to-bust, can be stitched in a single run. Others, like bust-to-waist-to-hip, need more than one stitching run.

We always stitch from the fullest part of the suppression before 'running off' at the smallest part. Don't worry if this sounds a bit confusing, it will become clearer in the next exercise.

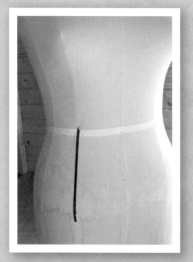

WAIST-TO-HIP

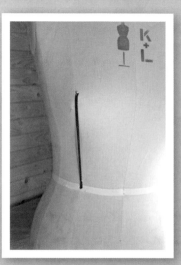

WAIST-TO-BUST

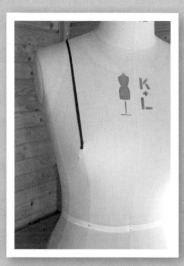

SHOULDER-TO-BUST

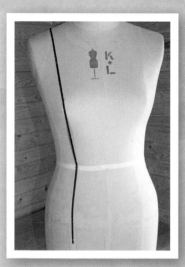

SHOULDER-
TO-BUST-TO-
WAIST-TO-HIP

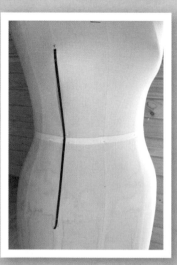

BUST-TO-
WAIST-TO-HIP

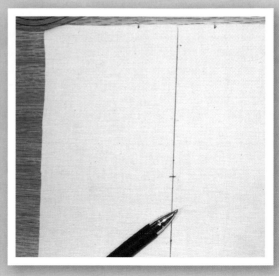

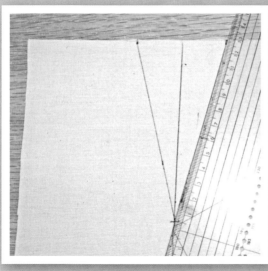

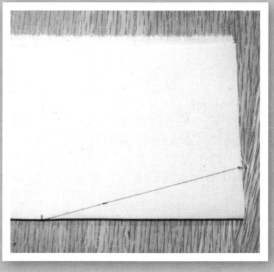

A single-run dart

1 Rule a line down the centre of a square of calico, and make a mark half-way down.

2 Now measure about 1¼ inches (3cm) either side of the centre line at the top end of the fabric and make a mark.

3 Snip these marks and draw a line from the snip to the marked point on the centre.

4 Fold fabric in half along the centre line.

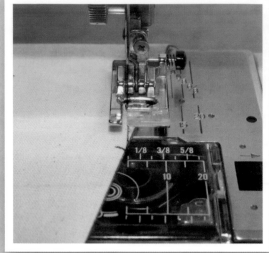

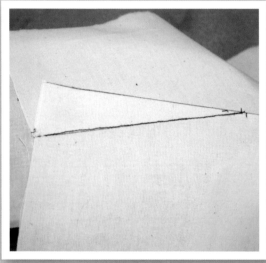

5 Matching up the snips, stitch along the marked line from the top edge to the middle.

6 Be sure to 'run off' the stitching at the end of the dart by letting the machine sew a few stitches beyond the edge of the fabric.

7 Cut the thread and tie the ends together to prevent the dart coming undone. Press it to one side using either a sleeve board or the pointed end of your ironing board.

8 Flip over to reveal the 'right side' of the fabric with a finished dart.

1

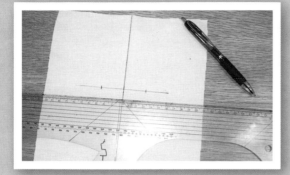

2

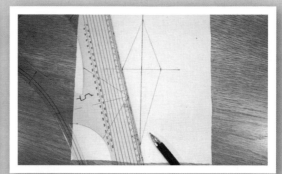

3

4a

4b

A multiple-dart run

1 Rule a line down the centre of a square of calico and make a mark half-way down. Using the designer's square, draw a line at right angles to the centre line and about 1¼ inches (3cm) either side.

2 Draw a dot on the centre line about 1½ inches (4cm) down from the top of the fabric and 1½ inches (4cm) up from the bottom. Connect the dots to mark the dart.

3 Fold fabric in half along the centre line.

4 Stitch along the dart lines, first from the centre to the top running off at the narrowest point (**4a**), then down from the centre to the bottom (**4b**).

5

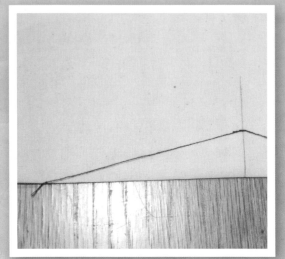

6a

6b

7

5 Run off the stitching as before.

6 Snip into the centre of the dart (**6a**), open up and press to one side (**6b**).

7 Turn the fabric over to the 'right side' to see your finished double dart.

Oh, how clever you are!

Seam Finishes

Seams are rarely finished off in couture sewing. Edges are usually 'bagged' inside the lining. You may, however, wish to neaten and finish off the seams just in case someone gets a glimpse inside.

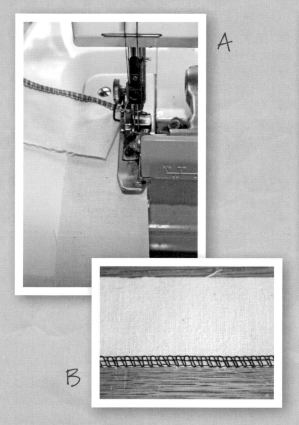

Overlocked edges

Overlockers are the neatest way to finish off a rough edge. They use either three or four threads that bind off the edge of the fabric, removing the rough edges as you sew (**A**).

When overlocking, take care not to trim off too much edge fabric. This can cut into your seam allowance and alter the size of the finished garment (**B**).

Overcasting

If you don't have access to an overlocker, you can use the zigzag setting on your machine with an overcast foot – see the instruction manual for guidance (**C**).

This is not as neat as an overlocked edge, but it's quite acceptable for the occasional straight seam (**D**).

1

2

3a

3b

French seam

On a long straight seam, such as on a long skirt, the French seam is by far my favourite method of finishing. It is very neat, adds strength and body, as well as working like a 'double seam' to lock in any of the raw edges.

1 Take two long strips of waste fabric.

2 Place the 'wrong sides' of the fabric together (the sides that will face the inside of your garment).

3 Stitch down the seam line using a ¼ inch (0.5cm) seam allowance (**3a & 3b**).

4a

4b

5a

5b

6

4 Press the seam open (**4a**) then fold the right sides together (the raw edges will be on the inside) and press again (**4b**).

5 Now stitch down the pressed edge using a ⅜ inch (1cm) seam allowance, trapping the first seam inside – it sounds much more complicated than it actually is! (**5a & 5b**)

6 Now press the finished seam to one side.

Hems

A badly turned hem can ruin a beautiful dress. Think of it as wearing hoop earrings with a classic Dior evening gown. This section looks at simple but very effective methods of hem finishing.

The traditional hem

You may have been expecting to use the turned-up, then hand- or machine-stitched hem. In fact, this is the type of hem I use least as it is by far the easiest to get wrong.

You can often see the pressing line on the 'right side', and any visible stitches or puckers will stand out like a sore thumb. Here are some pleasant alternatives.

The bagged-in hem

The bagged-in hem (**A**) is probably the simplest hemline finish. It is made by cutting out a lining the same length as the skirt, stitching round the hem and turning it through before sewing the skirt to the bodice. This hides all the seam edges but adds bulk to the finished garment. It also works well on both full or straight skirts, and for either short or long designs.

A

A

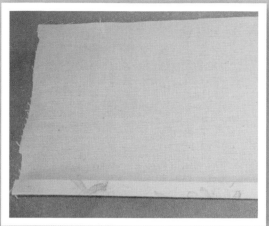

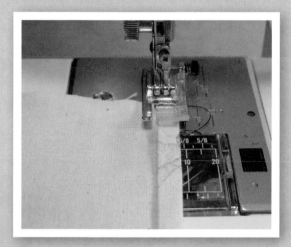

C

D

The roll-turned hem

The roll-turned hem is suitable for linings and underskirts.

Press the hem ½ inch (1cm) to the inside (**A**), then turn it down again by ¼ inch (0.5cm) making a double turn (**B**).

Sew on the wrong side, as close to the turned edge as possible (**C**), then press to form a neat finish (**D**).

The bias-bagged hem

This is a really nice hem finish. It adds weight and body to a hem line and, as there is a seam line at the edge rather than a fold, is very neat. It can be used on any shaped hem and is useful for curved hems such as those on full-circle skirts. Some hand sewing is required so it is sensible to practise many times to develop confidence.

To make bias strips

You can buy cotton or satin bias binding, but it looks much nicer made from the main fabric of the garment – and it's also very easy to do.

1 Lay out the fabric and rule 2 inch (5cm) lines at 45-degree angles across the fabric.

2 Cut along lines, lay the ends of two strips together at right angles and stitch. Repeat for the other pieces, stitching together to make one long strip, then press (**2a & 2b**).

3 Fold widthways by ¼ inch (0.5cm) and press. This will be the edge that you hand sew in place.

4 Next you need to take a practice strip of fabric about 4 inches (10cm) wide. With the 'right sides' together, stitch the unpressed edge of the bias strip to the edge of the practice piece using a ¼ inch (0.5cm) seam allowance (**4a–4d**).

4c

4d

5a

5b

5c

6

5 Press the seam open, then fold the bias strip to the wrong side and press again (**5a**). Hand sew in place, catching just one thread on the main fabric with each stitch (**5b & 5c**).

6 Press again.

Useful Tip

The right side of a fabric is the one that will face outwards on the finished garment. With patterned fabrics, for example, this will be the clear, brightly coloured side.

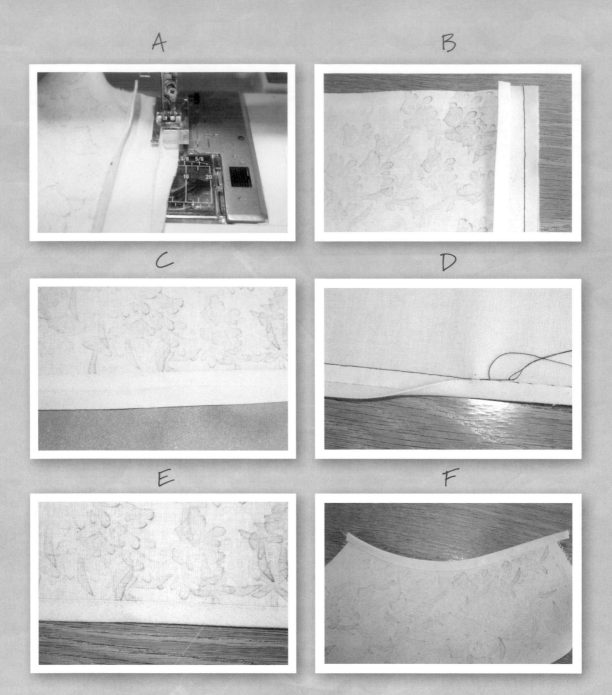

A

B

C

D

E

F

The bias-bound hem

Prepare the bias strips as for the previous exercise. Using a ¼ inch (0.5cm) seam allowance, sew the unfolded edge to the edge you want to finish. Turn the folded edge of the bias strip to the inside and hand-sew in place along the stitching line. This will bind the edge (**A– E**).

This technique is useful for finishing all sorts of edges, hems, armholes, necklines and so on. As the strip is cut on the bias or cross grain, it will stretch and shrink easily and works well with curved seams (**F**).

Boned Seams

There are times when you want to add stiffness and support to seams, such as on a basque top or a corset. Adding boning to a seam is not as difficult as it may sound. Just take this section slowly, and you might just dazzle yourself with the results.

In the past boning was made from whale bones, but it is now produced from many different materials including steel, solid polyester and (my choice) rigiline, which is made from thin strands of polyester and nylon woven together. While other types of boning slot inside a casing, rigiline is sewn directly on to the seam.

Useful Tip

As well as boning seams, you can add stiffness to any part of a garment – such as shirt collars, hooped skirts and so on.

1 Run a seam down a scrap piece of fabric and press it open.

Now set your machine to the zigzag setting and cut a length of rigiline the same length as the seam.

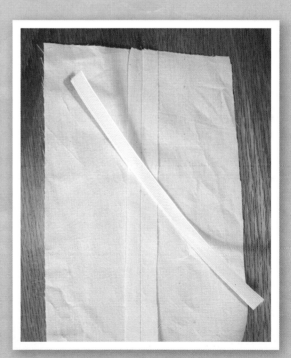

1

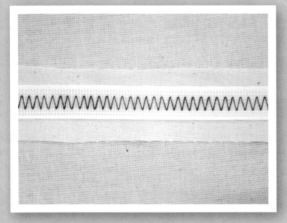

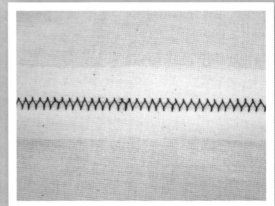

2 The ends of boning can be sharp and may poke through the main garment, so it is important to wrap the ends. Cut small squares of scrap fabric and place a square over the end of the bone.

3 Lay boning along the seam line on the 'wrong side' and zigzag down, taking care to stay over the stitching line (**3a–c**). Finish by placing another square of scrap fabric over the end of the bone.

Fastenings

In much the same way as hems, badly inserted fastenings can spoil otherwise elegant and beautifully finished garments. Paying attention to detail pays off! This section explores a number of different fastenings – from zips to rouleau loops.

Zips

The easiest but best-looking fastening of all is the concealed zip; from the outside it looks like another seam. Concealed zips are slightly different from normal zips as the slider is on the opposite side.

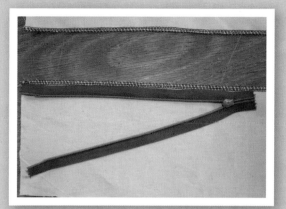

1

To insert a concealed zip

As with many other sewing techniques in this book, this process is much simpler than it seems. As soon as you have added an 'invisible' zip, you will understand the principle and never use a normal zip again.

Buy a few 8 or 10 inch (20 or 25cm) concealed zips from your local sewing shop, remembering that they are different from normal zips.

1 Take two pieces of scrap fabric and place onto the table with the 'right sides' facing up. Now undo the zip. The right side (front) actually looks more like the wrong side (back) of the zip.

With the wrong side up, open the zip fully and place the right-hand tape on the left piece of fabric. Make sure the end of the tape is at the top of the fabric.

You will find that you can roll open the 'teeth' on the wrong side of the zip just by holding the tape flat to the fabric with your right hand, and rolling the teeth to the left. We are going to sew in this crease line.

2

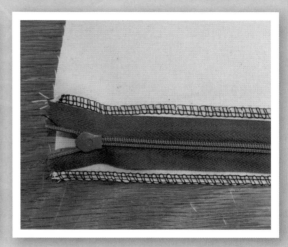

3

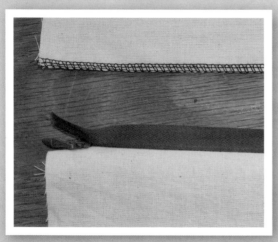

4

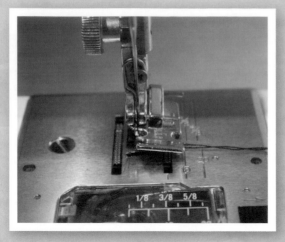

5

2 Attach the zip foot to the machine (see manufacturer's instructions) so the needle is on the left side of the foot.'

3 With the edge of the zip tape ¼ inch (0.5cm) in from the edge of the fabric, roll open the 'teeth' slightly. Now, stitching in the crease line, sew down to about ¾ inch (2cm) from the 'stop staple' at the bottom of the zip. Remember to do a lock stitch at the start and end.

4 Close the zip. Tuck the seam under, folding the zip tape to the 'wrong side' of the fabric. Place it alongside the second piece of the fabric and flip it over so that the right sides of the fabric are together.

5 Undo the zip.

6

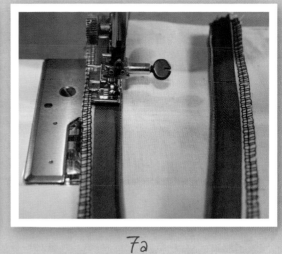

7a

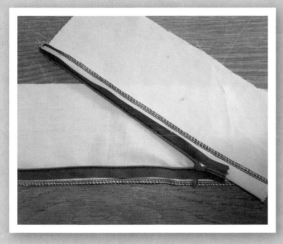

7b

8

6 Move the zip foot so that the needle is on the right-hand side of the foot.

7 Sew down the zip tape, just as for the first side (step 3), making sure you stop ¾ inch (2cm) from the 'stop staple' at the bottom of the zip (**7a & 7b**).

8 Open up the work so that the 'right side' is facing up. Now do up the zip so that it looks like a normal seam.

9

10a

10b

11

9 Fold all the fabric, right sides together, and leaving the zip foot in the same position, stitch down from where the stitching line stops.

Avoid catching the zip tape by folding the zip in half and pulling it slightly out of the way as you stitch down.

10 Press the seam open on the wrong side of the fabric and press over the zip on the right side (**10a & 10b**).

11 Insert several zips using this technique until you are confident with the procedure.

Buttons and Rouleau Loops

A rouleau is a thin strip of bias-cut fabric that is seamed down one side, then turned through to make a 'tube'. These are often used as loops for buttons or lacing, as well as for straps on tops, dresses and lingerie.

Buttons and loops create a very nice effect, especially when you place the buttons close together. You can place a row of buttons and loops down the back of a dress, a few on a cuff or one as a back neck fastening.

1a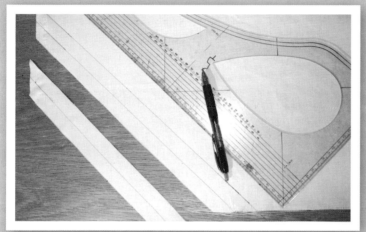

1b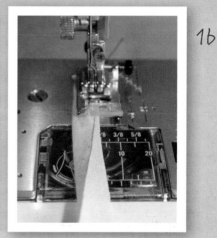

2a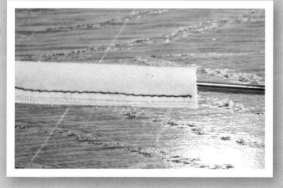

2b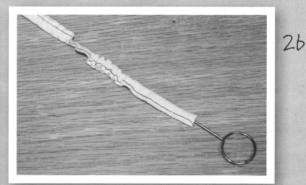

How to make rouleau loops

1 Lay out the fabric and mark ¾ inch (2cm) bias strips. Cut out the strips then, working each one in turn, fold in half along width. Stitch in from the folded edge, using a ¼ inch (0.5cm) seam allowance (**1a & 1b**).

2 Using a rouleau hook (a thin length of wire with a loop at one end and a latch-hook at the other) push the hook end inside the rouleau and grab the top end of the rouleau (**2a & 2b**).

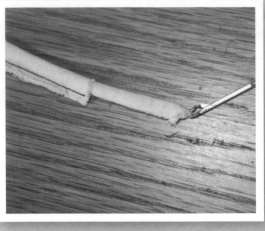

3a

3b

4a

4b

3 Very slowly and carefully pull through by turning the rouleau right side out (**3a & 3b**).

4 Take a button of the required size and measure around the circumference. Add 1¼ inches (3cm) to this figure and you will have the precise measurement for cutting your rouleau loops (**4a & 4b**).

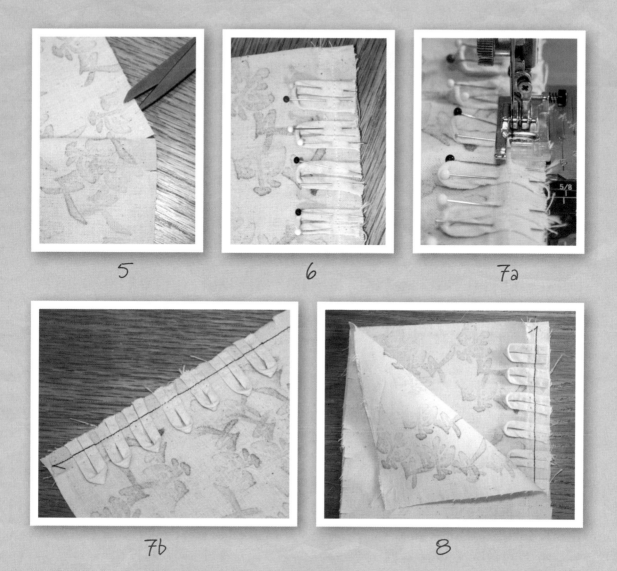

5

6

7a

7b

8

5 Cut two strips of waste fabric to a width of 4 inches (10cm). Notch markings down one side, ¾ inch (2cm) apart.

6 Fold one rouleau loop in half, line up the raw edges with the edge of your fabric (right side up) on the notched mark and pin them in place.

7 When all loops are in position, run a line of stitching ⅜ inch (1cm) in from the edge of the fabric to secure (**7a & 7b**).

8 Remove pins. Place the second strip of fabric over the first with the 'right sides' together. This is called the 'facing' – it traps all the loops in between the two layers of fabric.

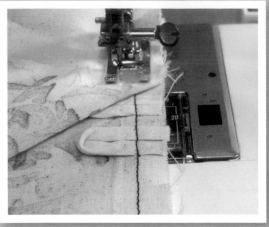

9

10a

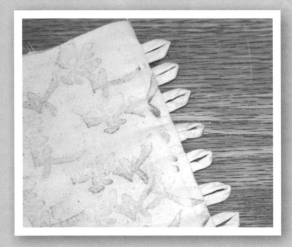

10b.

11a

9 Stitch down the fabric using a ⅝ inch (1.5cm) seam allowance.

10 Fold the 'facing' around to the back of the work, exposing the loops, before pressing (**10a & 10b**).

11 'Face' a second strip of fabric – as in the previous step, but without the rouleau loops – and press. Lay the looped and plain pieces side by side and sew on the buttons to correspond with the loops (**11a & 11b**).

11b

Lacing

Lacing up the back of a corset or basque top can be a very effective technique. It allows a little ease for fitting a garment, as it can be laced either looser or tighter depending on the wearer.

Lacing works best on boned garments, but is sometimes used to fasten skirts or cuffs. Holes or eyelets must be made in a fabric to thread the lacing through, and there are several ways to do this. Eyelets and tools for applying them directly to fabric are available from haberdashery stores, but this often splits the fabric and the holes can fray so I tend not to use this method.

Eyelet tape, which has strong eyelet holes already made, is also available. It is quite effective on corsets, but I would only use this method if the tape will not show on the finished garment.

The third method of lacing, which I prefer, is to use rouleau loops and ribbon or lacing cord. Apply the loops, but don't make them as long as you did in the previous exercise. Ensure that the loops are evenly spaced and that you have the same number on both sides. Lace up with cord (**A & B**).

 A
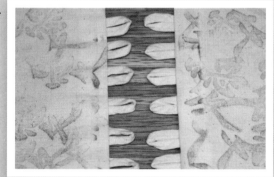

B
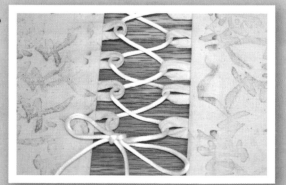

That's pretty much all the sewing techniques you will need to sew your very own, fabulous party dress. Now we're ready to get started.

At this stage, it is advisable to go back and re-do any exercises that you didn't feel comfortable with. Make sure that you are confident using all of the techniques before you go any further.

Over the next few pages we'll look at how to make a pattern.

Making the Blocks

'Your dresses should be tight enough to show you're a woman and loose enough to show you're a lady.'

EDITH HEAD

The Body Block

A body block is a fabric rendition of half your exact body shape. It is the starting point for a pattern and is very important in regards to fitting your dress perfectly. Get this part right and it will save you a lot of time adjusting the toile later.

You won't be able to create a body block on your own. Find a sewing partner to help.

You will need:

- A tape measure
- A designer's square
- Calico
- Marker pen with a fine tip
- Pins
- Elastic
- A spirit level – this isn't essential but helps if you can't line things up by eye
- A very tight-fitting white t-shirt (buy a size too small so it fits very tightly). Fold the t-shirt in half (**A**) down the centre front and draw a line (**B**) with your felt-tip pen to mark. Do the same (**C**) down the centre back.

You will now need to take seven measurements:

- Bust
- Hips
- Nape of neck to just below the buttocks
- Bust point to bust point (nipple to nipple)
- Shoulder blade to shoulder blade
- Above shoulder to bust point
- Above shoulder to shoulder blade point.

Write these measurements down carefully

Important note:

If your hip measurement is larger than your bust measurement, you will have to make a separate bodice block and skirt block. Follow the instructions for the bodice to the waist, then do the same for the skirt. When you have finished, join the bodice pieces to the corresponding skirt pieces.

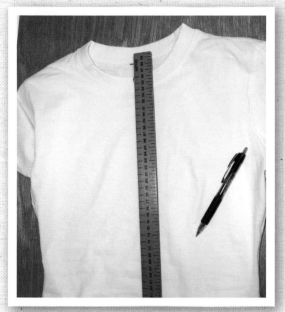

A

B

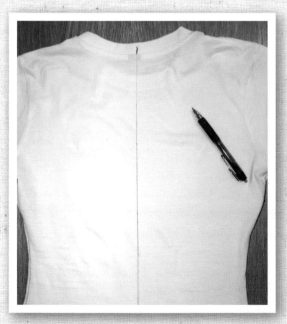

C

Useful Tip

A toile is a mock-up of the actual dress, which will be unpicked to form the pattern for the real thing.

1a

1b

2

TOP BACK

TOP FRONT

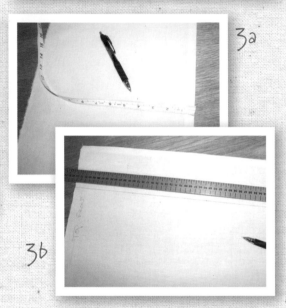

3a

3b

1 Cut two strips of calico, ¼ of the bust or hip measurement (the larger of the two) plus 4 inches (10cm) in width, by the measurement from the nape of the neck to below the buttock plus 4 inches (10cm) in length (**1a**). Fold back ⅜ inch (1cm) of fabric down one of the long edges of each piece of calico and press (**1b**).

2 Place the two strips down with the turn of the left piece on the left side and the turn of the right piece on the right. Write 'top' on the top edge of both pieces, 'front' on the right piece and 'back' on the left.

3 Working with the front piece, measure in from the folded edge (**3a**) by half of the nipple-to-nipple measurement.

Do this in a couple of places and draw a line through the points, making sure it is parallel to the folded edge of the fabric (**3b**). If you are modelling the top and skirt separately, you also need to measure the same amount in from the skirt centre front.

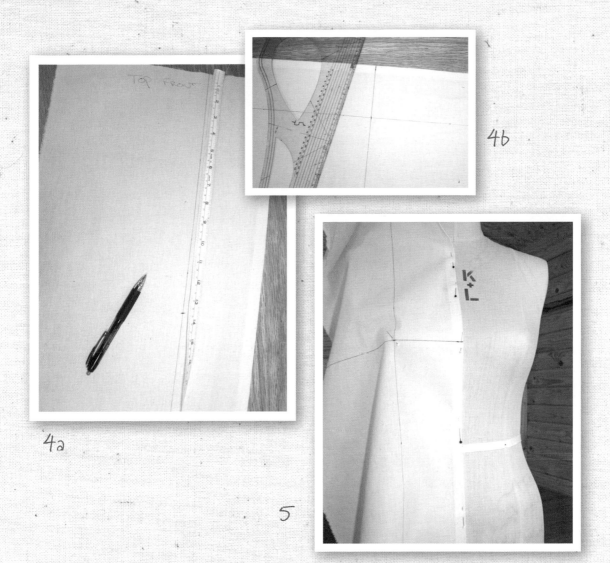

4a

4b

5

4 Now measure down from the top of this line – the above-shoulder-to-bust-point measurement – and mark (**4a**). This will be your bust point.

Using the designer's square, draw a line at right angles to the first line cutting through the bust point mark (**4b**).

5 Pin the bust-point mark to the model's bust-point (be very careful) then pin the folded edge to the centre line on the t-shirt, keeping the bust line horizontal.

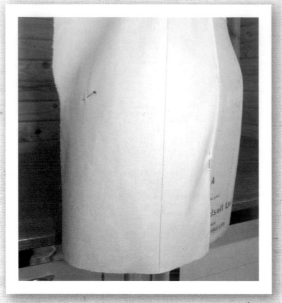

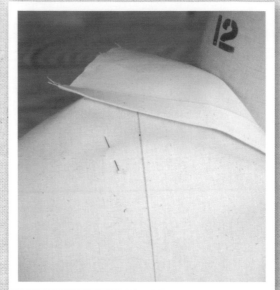

8a

8b

6 With the flat of your hand, smooth the fabric across the hip and pin at the side.

7 Smooth the fabric up from the bust and pin to just below the shoulder.

8 Now mark in the neckline using sharp scissors. Taking care not to cut your model, point the scissors upwards with the points to the left of the neckline and snip up (**8a**). This will free up some of the fabric, making it sit closer to the body (**8b**).

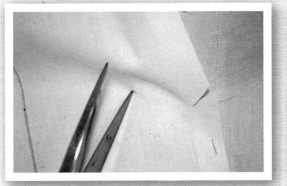

9a

9b

9c

10a

10b

9 Continue this method all around the neck to the shoulder seam (**9a–c**).

10 Now that the block sits close to the neck, mark around the neck shape and cut away any excess fabric. Pin to hold at the neck edge of the shoulder (**10a & 10b**).

Making the Blocks   59

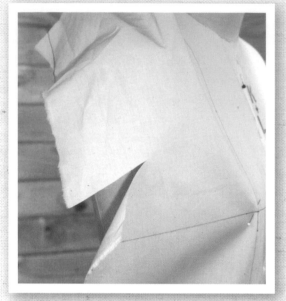

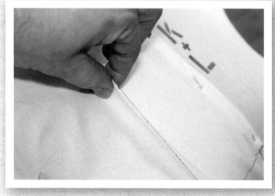

11 Now insert the shoulder-to-bust-point dart. Cut a line from the side seam, close to the armpit, to the armhole seam on the t-shirt; this will free up some of the fabric.

12 Look at the bust line and straighten it so it runs absolutely horizontal – it may be easier to use a spirit level here – and pin the line to the side seam.

13 Take out the pin holding the block up at the shoulder. With the flat of your hand, smooth the fabric upwards from the bust. Fold fabric along the vertical line and pin the resulting dart in place as close to the body as possible without stretching the t-shirt. Pin to hold the shoulder in place. (**13a & 13b**).

Note: You can pin in this dart anywhere on the shoulder but, for now, centre it on the line drawn in earlier. For very full-busted models, just pin the dart in where the most natural fall of the fabric seems to be.

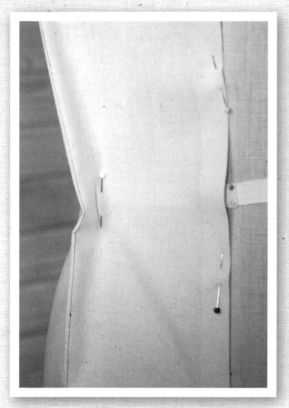

14a

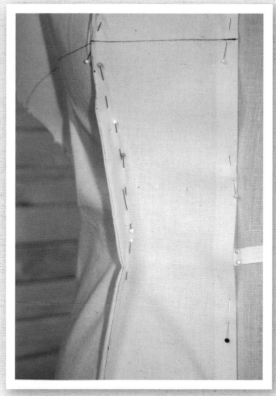

14b

15

14 We are now going to suppress the waist dart up to the bust and down to the hip. Folding on the line – as we did with the bust dart – pin out the fullness at the waist. (**14a & 14b**).

15 Carry on up to the bust point, then down to the hip in the same way. Fit close to the body but take care not to stretch the t-shirt. If you are modelling a separate top and skirt block, model only the waist and make the skirt as a separate piece later.

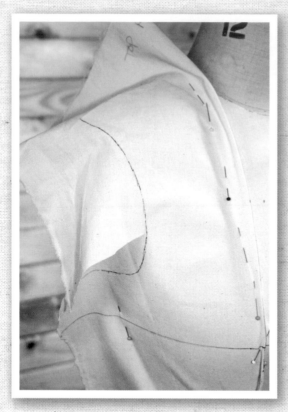

16a

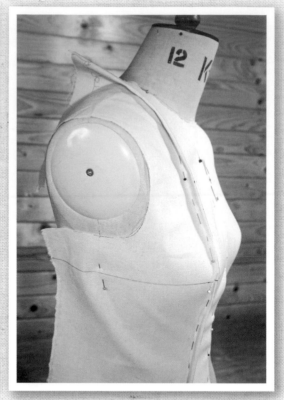

16b

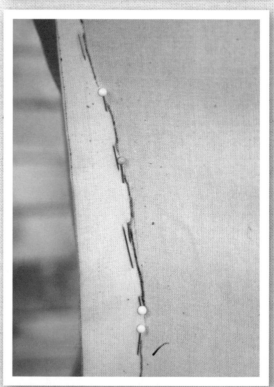

17

16 Mark around the armhole seam – from the edge of the shoulder to the underarm – and trim away any excess fabric (**16a & 16b**).

17 Mark in both sides of all the darts, following the pin lines.

The front block is finished for the time being. We will now repeat the process, in the same order, on the back block.

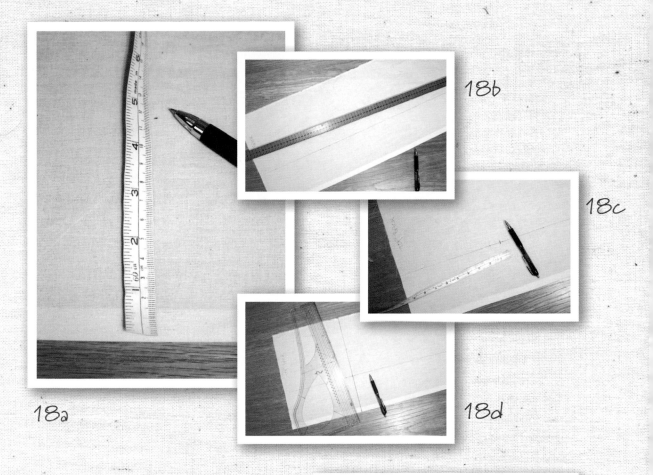

18a

18b

18c

18d

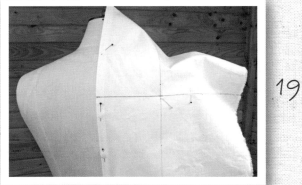

19

18 Take the back piece that we cut earlier. Measure in the blade-to-blade measurement from the folded edge of the fabric and make a mark (**18a**).

Draw a line parallel to the folded edge running through this mark (**18b**).

Measure down this line from the top – the above-shoulder-to-blade measurement – and mark; this is the blade point (**18c**).

Draw a line at right angles to the first line, cutting through the blade point (**18d**).

19 Pin the blade point to the shoulder blade and the centre back to the centre-back line on the t-shirt. Insert a pin to hold the shoulder line up, making sure the blade line is horizontal. Smooth the fabric out to the hip and pin at the side seam.

20a

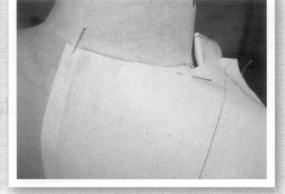

20b

21a

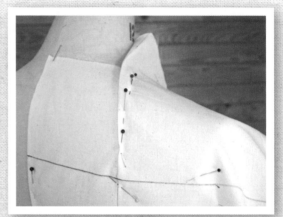

21b

20 Snip into the back neckline as for the front; mark and trim (**20a**). Pin the fabric at the neck edge of the shoulder (**20b**).

21 Cut in from the side seam – close to the armpit – right up to the armhole seam on the t-shirt (**21a**).

Pin under the arm, keeping the blade line horizontal. Smooth the fabric upwards and pin out the shoulder dart (**21b**).

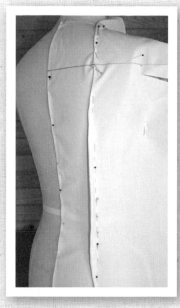

24

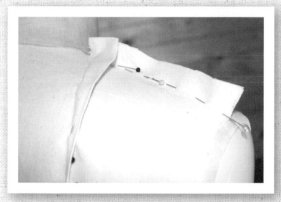

22 Pin out the waist dart just as for the front, up to the blade point and down to the hip. If you are modelling a separate top and skirt, do this on separate pieces (**22a & 22b**).

23 Mark the armhole, following the armhole seam on the t-shirt, and cut away any excess fabric.

24 Pin in the shoulder line, pinning the back to the front and keeping as close to the shoulder as you can. Trim away the extra fabric.

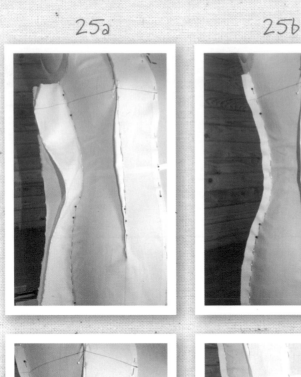

25a

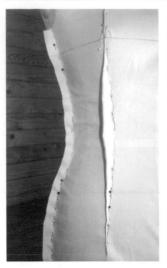

25b

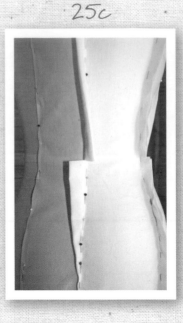

25c

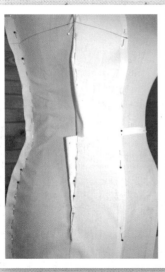

25d

26a

26b

25 With the model's arm bent and slightly out to the side – and the elbow in line with the slope of the shoulder – remove the pins at the hips and underarm.

Pin the side seams in, keeping as close to the body as you possibly can without stretching the t-shirt (**25a**). Cut away any excess fabric (**25b**).

Mark in both sides of all darts, as for the front. Snip into the waist darts to relax the fabric ever so slightly – this step isn't necessary if you are making a separate top and skirt block (**25c & 25d**).

26 Tie a length of elastic around the waist, another round the hips and one close to the bottom of your block (**26a & 26b**).

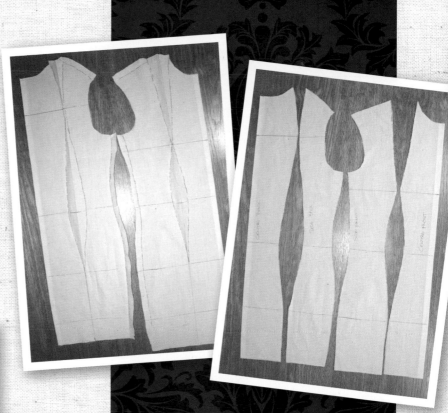

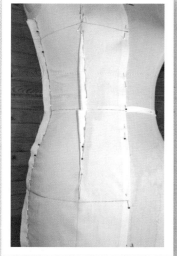

26c

Making sure that each piece of elastic is absolutely horizontal, mark lines around the body block using the elastics as guides – use your spirit level if you need to (**26c**).

You have now finished half of the block modelling. Remove the block from your model and take out the pins. If you have ever used a purchased paper pattern, this will look very familiar.

Take out all the pins and cut on the dart and seam lines. You will now have four pattern pieces: centre front, side front, side back and centre back. If you are modelling the blocks separately, join the top pieces to the corresponding skirt pieces using sticky tape. Mark the piece names on the block.

We are now going to make and fit a full body block from these pattern pieces.

Full Block

Your body block is the key to creating a beautifully fitting party dress. Don't carry on to the next stage of the design process until you've made one that fits you perfectly. It's worth taking the time to get this critical stage of the process right.

Before we start, I need to say a few words about fabric grain. The threads of a fabric run top to bottom and side to side. To give the garment structure and body, always cut along on the 'straight grain'. To make a garment soft and draped, cut along the 'cross grain' or bias – this runs diagonally across the grain. Cross or bias cutting can be very difficult; as the sewing techniques are too advanced for beginners, they have not been explored in this book.

Let's start to cut and sew.

Before doing anything, make sure the calico isn't creased. I always press fabric before starting a project.

1

Useful Tip

The selvedge is the edge of the fabric that is woven to prevent unravelling.

Fold a piece of calico – long enough to fit all your body block pieces – in half across the width. Fold the selvedge to the selvedge so that the fold will be on the 'straight grain'.

1 Lay the folded fabric out on your cutting area – a table or, if you don't have room, the floor – with the folded edge towards you. Lay the folded edge of the centre-front piece along the fold of the fabric and pin in place.

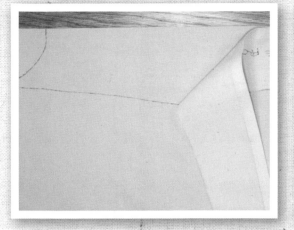

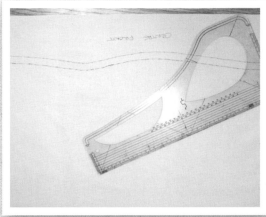

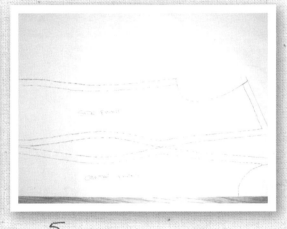

2 Mark round the pattern piece before removing it from the fabric.

3 We now need to add a seam allowance. Using the designer's square, mark ⅝ inch (1.5cm) outside the pattern piece on the side and the shoulder seams.

4 Draw a line at right angles to the fold line of the calico, level with the hip line on the centre-front block piece. Place the side-front pattern piece next to the centre-front piece, with the hip line running along the one you just drew in. This will make sure the pattern piece sits on the straight grain of the fabric.

5 Leave room for the seam allowance, mark around it, and then add a seam allowance to the shoulder and side seams.

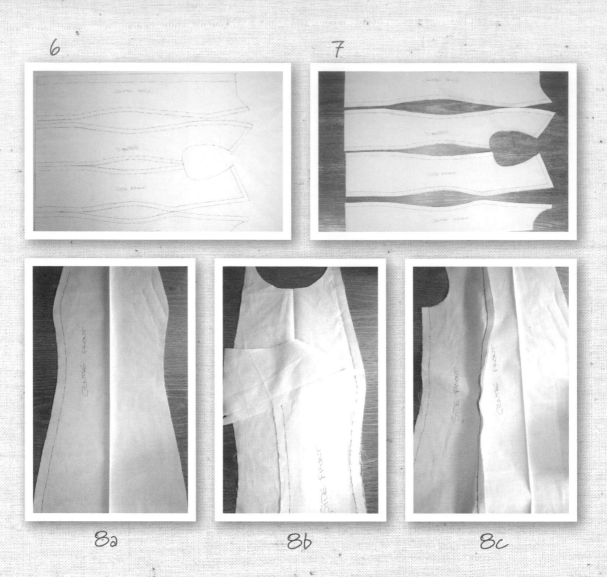

6

7

8a

8b

8c

6 Repeat for the side-back and centre-back pieces, placing the hip line on the line already drawn in – as before. Add a 1¼ inch (3cm) seam to the centre-back line to provide a little room to pin. As with your half block, add a label to each piece.

It doesn't matter if you can't manage to lay the pieces side by side, but it saves on fabric if you can. It is important to make sure that the pattern pieces are on the 'straight grain' of the fabric.

7 Cut out the block pieces on the lines. Now we are going to sew the pieces together to form the body block. Don't use a locking stitch at the beginning or end of the seams as we are going to undo them later.

8 Take the centre-front piece, open it up and place the side front, bust line seams and right sides together (**8a–c**). You will be stitching along the first line drawn onto the half block (page 56). Matching the stitching lines, sew a ⅝ inch (1.5cm) seam from the shoulder edge to hip edge.

9

10a

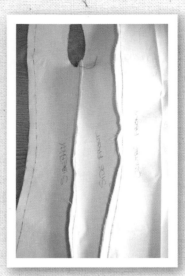

10b

11a

11b

9 Repeat with the second side-front piece.

10 With right sides together, place the side-back and side-front seams together and sew, starting from under the arm down to the hip (**10a & 10b**). Repeat this process for the other side-back piece.

11 Now take the centre-back pieces and, with right sides together, sew down from the shoulder to the hip (**11a & 11b**).

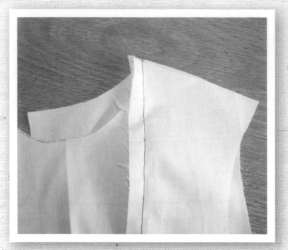

Now take the right-hand shoulder seams, making sure the right sides are placed together, and sew (**12a & 12b**). Do the same for the other shoulder.

Finally, snip into the curved seams and press to complete the block (**13a & 13b**).

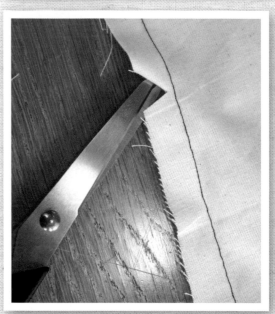

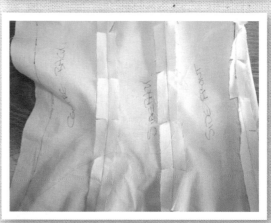

14a

14b

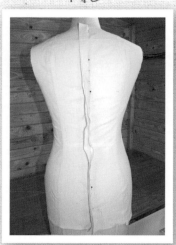

14c

Fitting the body block

Unless you're a contortionist, you'll need some help when fitting the body block. Try it on, wearing foundation garments rather than the t-shirt; it should fit the body tightly. Pin down the back seam as close to the body as you can, taking care not to pull or stretch the block. If everything works as it should, the pinning line will be on the line you drew on the centre back (**14a–c**).

Look closely at the way the block fits. Is the fabric bunching up anywhere?

If the fit isn't perfect, pin down the wrinkles and creases before marking. Unpick your block on the seams – leaving the new pins in – and re-mark, sewing a new body block from this one. Remember that the seam allowance is already marked so it shouldn't take as long this time.

Try it on again. This time it will fit like a glove. I told you it was worth taking the time to get it right!

Left
TOO MUCH FULLNESS
OVER BUST

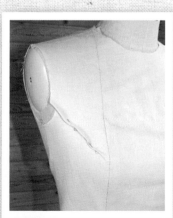

Right
FULLNESS PINNED OUT

The Basic Boned Bodice

We have now covered most of the sewing techniques you will need to make your party dress. This exercise covers the techniques used to produce a basic boned bodice, used in two of the dresses in this book.

The laced-up bodice or basque is very fashionable at the moment, and two of the four dresses in this book use a basic basque construction as a foundation. For your basque, choose a very tightly woven fabric such as a brocade or heavy silk.

You will need:

- 1½ yards (1.5 metres) of main fabric
- 1 yard (1 metre) of calico for the interlining
- Calico for the new body block and toile
- 1 yard (1 metre) of coordinating lining fabric
- 3 yards (3 metres) of rigiline polyester boning
- 5 yards (5 metres) corset lacing or ribbon.

Useful Tip

The basque takes such a small amount of main fabric that I lined it using the same fabric. I'll leave the choice up to you.

First, make the pattern. Take the body block you just made and undo all the stitching carefully using a seam ripper. Press the pieces flat using a little spray starch to stabilize them.

Press the centre-front piece in half, side seam to side seam, and cut carefully down the fold line. Take one half of this centre-front, one side-front, one side-back and one centre-back piece. Put the other half of the body block aside to use another time. Remember that seam allowances are already included.

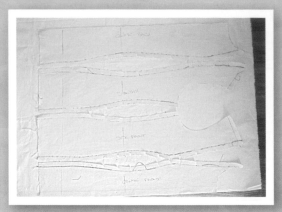

1a

1b

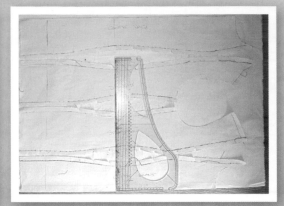

2

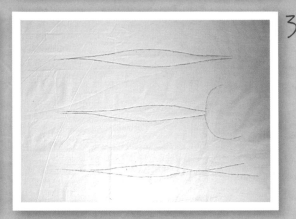

3a

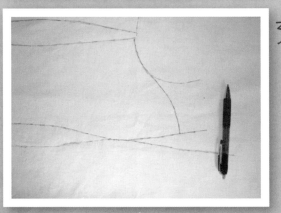

3b

1 Lay out the pattern pieces to the fold of the calico just as when you made the body block. Make sure the waist line of the pattern is at 90 degrees to the fold line using the designer's set square. This will ensure that the pattern pieces are on the straight grain of the fabric (**1a & 1b**).

2 Draw round the pattern pieces. Don't bother to go all the way up to the shoulders or down to the bottom of the block as these areas will not be used.

3 Now draw in the top line, starting under the arm and continuing in a nice curve up to an appropriate level above the bust point (**3a & 3b**). You don't want any unfortunate 'pop out' accidents, do you?

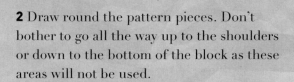

The Party Dress

4a

4b

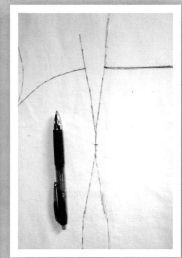

5

4 Measure up from the bust point to your top line. Swing the tape over and mark in the same measurement up from the bust point (**4a & 4b**).

5 Draw in the centre top line from the mark. Angle this up, down, or go straight across as shown – it's up to you.

6 Draw in the top back line from under the arm, curving down slightly (**6a**). With the aid of the set square, continue this at right angles to the centre-back seam (**6b**).

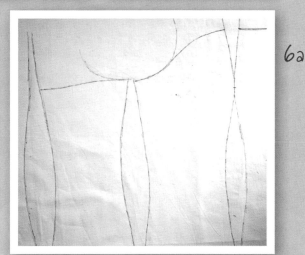

6a

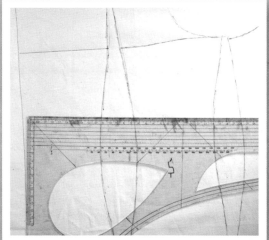

6b

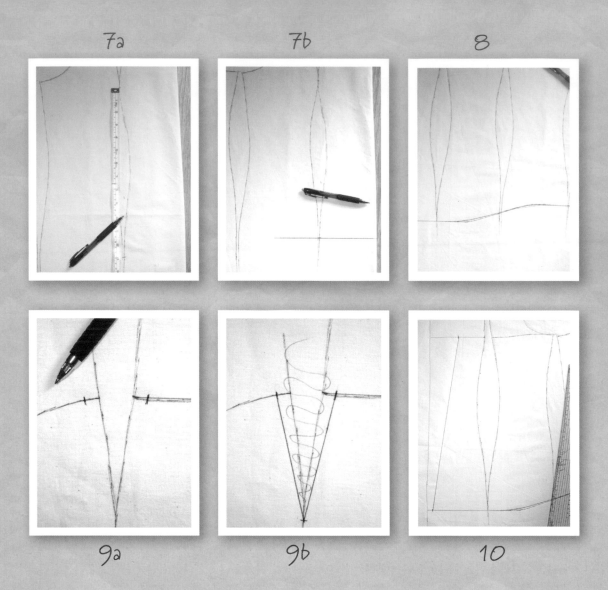

7a

7b

8

9a

9b

10

7 Measure from your own bust point to decide where you want your basque to end – somewhere between waist and hips is about right. Transfer this measurement to the pattern, measuring down from the bust point, and make a mark. Draw in the bottom line at right angles to the centre front (**7a & 7b**).

8 Start to curve the line down slightly towards the hips, and carry on to the centre back, making sure the bottom line is at right angles to the centre-back line.

9 To make sure the top of the basque fits very closely to the body, mark in points about ⅜ inch (1cm) in from both sides of the bust seam. Connect these up to the bust point, scribbling out the original lines to prevent confusion (**9a & 9b**).

10 Look at the shape of the back seam. Mark about ¾ inch (1.5cm) in from the bottom edge, and 2 inches (5cm) from the top edge to leave room for the lacing. Connect the marks and add a ⅝ inch (1.5cm) seam allowance to this line.

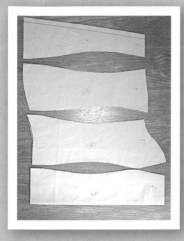

11a

11b

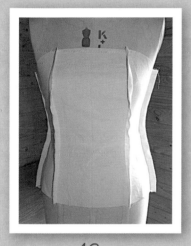

12a

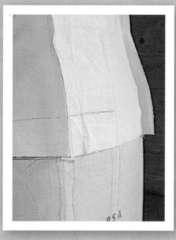

12b

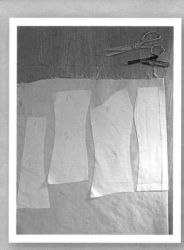

13

11 Cut out the pattern pieces, marking them as for the body block. Indicate the top with arrows to remind you how to place them on the fabric. Sew the toile together in the same order as for the body block (**11a & 11b**).

12 Try on the toile, remembering that you left room for the lacing. Look at the fit and proportion carefully and mark any changes needed. In this case the basque was too long, so a new bottom line was marked in, still sloping slightly down towards the back (**12a & 12b**).

13 Undo, press and starch the pattern pieces. Cut out the main fabric, lining and calico interlining separately, placing the centre front to the fold. Don't try to cut all three at once as the fabric may slip and you won't get a good fit or finish.

14a

14b

15

16a

16b

17a

17b

15 Bone the seams of the interlining, covering both ends of the rigiline with small pieces of scrap fabric. Add an extra bone to the centre front seam for a little more support if you like (**15**).

16 You now have three separate basques in main fabric, interlining and lining. Place the main fabric and interlining wrong sides together, with the seams and the bones on the inside (**16a & 16b**).

14 Join the pieces of the interlining in the same order as for the full body block. Snip into the curved seams and press them open. Repeat with the main fabric and the lining (**14a & 14b**).

17 Stitch a line ⅜ inch (1cm) in from both sides of the centre-back seam to hold the layers together during construction (this is sometimes called basting). Place a row of pins a little way in from the edge to keep the interlining out of the way during the next step (**17a & 17b**).

18a

18b

19

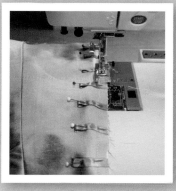

20a

20b

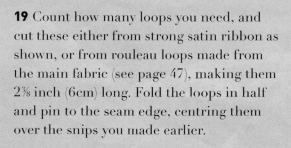

21a

21b

18 Mark the position of the loops for the lacing on both centre-back seams by snipping into the fabric edge, taking care to stay inside the seam allowances. Begin ⅜ inch (1cm) down from the top of the basque, then snip at intervals of 1 inch (2.5cm) down to the bottom edge. Make sure the snips match up exactly (**18a & 18b**).

19 Count how many loops you need, and cut these either from strong satin ribbon as shown, or from rouleau loops made from the main fabric (see page 47), making them 2⅜ inch (6cm) long. Fold the loops in half and pin to the seam edge, centring them over the snips you made earlier.

20 Sew over this seam to hold the loops in place. If you go slowly, you can quite happily sew over the pins (**20a & 20b**).

21 Place the lining over the main piece, right sides together and making sure it is the right way up. Join both centre-back seams using a ⅝ inch (1.5cm) seam allowance (**21a & 21b**).

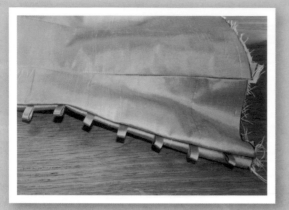

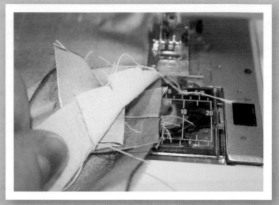

22 Turn the pieces to the right side – the loops will be trapped between the layers of fabric (**22a**). Stitch a line ⅜ inch (1cm) in from both the top and bottom edges to hold the layers together while you bind the edges (**22b**). Make sure all the layers line up and that all the seams match.

23 From the main fabric, cut two bias strips long enough to stretch from edge to edge of your basque with a small amount left over at each end. Pin the end loops out of the way so you do not catch them when you apply the binding (**23a & 23b**).

24 Take the binding and, with right sides together, fold ¾ inch (2cm) or so round to the back. Hold the binding in place and place under the machine. Stitch across the top seam, using a ⅜ inch (1cm) seam allowance and stopping about 4 inches (10cm) short of the end (**24a & 24b**).

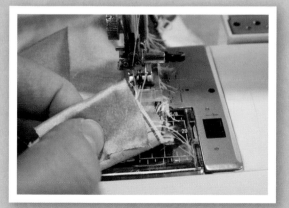

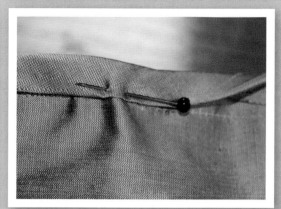

25 Trim the bias down to ¾ inch (2cm) past the end of the top of the basque. Fold under and finish the seam (**25a & 25b**).

26 Open up the bias binding, fold to the inside, pin and stitch in place by hand. As the ends were folded under before stitching the seam, they should be very tidy (**26a & 26b**).

27 Press the basque, lace it up using the ribbon you used for your loops (see page 81) or corset lacing. You're ready for a night on the town, but remember to put on a skirt or trousers first!

The Dresses

'Glamour is what makes a man ask for your telephone number and a woman ask for the number of your dress maker.'

LILLY DACHE

A Dress to Suit you

Now that you are equipped with a range of sewing techniques and have prepared your very own customized body block, it's time to move on to the exciting part – making your perfect party dress or gown.

Some of you may be eager to race ahead and make all the dresses in this book. Others may want to make just one, and see how they get on. If that's the case, make sure you choose a gown that suits you perfectly. The most important step in understanding what will flatter you is to identify your figure type.

I am constantly amazed that most women don't know their body shape. Read the body type descriptions in this section and be honest with yourself. Which category do you fit into? There's nothing wrong with any of the figure types, it's just a matter of proportion. If you know what type you are, you will also know the shapes that suit you. Play up your good bits!

Column
- Straight up and down, little size difference between bust, waist and hips.
- Tall and thin.
- Long rectangle shape.

Square
- Little variation between the bust, waist and hips.
- Shorter and fuller in figure than column body type.
- Square shape – no surprises there then!

Round
- Waist larger than hips and bust.
- Circle shape.

Top-heavy
- Very full in the bust with smaller waist and hips.
- Triangle shape.

Bottom-heavy
- Full in the hips and derrière and smaller in the bust and waist.
- Reverse triangle shape.

Hourglass
- Hips and bust about the same size, with a smaller waist.
- Figure eight shape.

Once you have identified your figure type, you need to know what shapes suit you. There are no hard and fast rules, but this exercise may encourage you to try something new. Remember, you don't wear a gown every day so be brave and make a statement.

If you are a Column

Aim to give the impression that your shoulders and hips are wider than they are, thereby cinching you in at the waist. Use a wide, scooped, round neckline and go for fuller skirt styles. Add boning to define the waist. Fit the bodice close to your body and wear a long sleeve with some fullness, or that gathers at the shoulder then narrows towards the wrist. Keep the shoe heel height fairly low.

If you are a Square

Try to lengthen your shape by wearing straight, almost pencil-style skirts in longer lengths. Try a wide 'v' neckline and plunge it as low as you dare. You can still get away with clothes that are quite fitted on the bodice. A sleeveless style works best, but if you prefer not to reveal the tops of your arms, wear a short or a three-quarter length fitted sleeve. Try a wide belt to pull you in at the waist.

If you are Round

Deceive the eye by giving the impression that you have a waist. Wear long, fitted skirt styles with a loose bodice and maybe a tie at the hips. Take inspiration from 20s- and 30s-style fashion. If you wear sleeves, make sure they are very fitted and full length. Square or 'v' necklines and cross-over styles work best.

If you are Top-heavy

Wear sleeveless tops with 'v' necklines that narrow your shoulders and widen your hips. Wrap-over styles work well, as do one-shoulder designs, but try not to add too many gathers to the bust area. Skirts should be full A-line, or full circle styles. Avoid wide belts as they will pull you in and exaggerate the size of your bust.

If you are Bottom-heavy

Wear round and scoop-shaped necklines to widen the top part of your body and a gathered short or long sleeve. Basque tops with sweetheart top lines and little sleeves also work well. Skirts are best fitted and just above ankle length. Wear high-heeled shoes whenever possible.

If you are an Hourglass

You lucky girls – you can wear just about anything! Consider your height – wear shorter lengths if you are tall and longer lengths if you are short. Look at fashion magazines and find shapes and styles that attract you. See if you can work out the pattern shapes and construction methods.

The Party Dress

Be Creative: Make your own Designs

The sewing techniques section includes some lessons that have not been used to make the gowns, so you will be able to devise your own designs beyond the ones in this book.

The four basic dress styles shown in this book will suit all figure types; the main thing to consider is proportion. The rule is simple: the fuller the figure, the longer and slimmer the dress should be, in order to lengthen and slim the overall shape. The slimmer the figure, the fuller the skirt styles can be.

But rules are made to be broken. You already know what suits you and the styles that you feel comfortable in. Show off your best features, and if you have a killer cleavage, let the world see it!

Using the design and sewing methods in this book, the starting point will always be your toile. Look at it carefully during your fittings and ask the following questions:

- Does it fit?
- Should it be longer or shorter?
- Should it be looser or tighter?
- Would it benefit from a lining? As well as hiding construction and raw seams, a good lining can smooth out any 'lumps and bumps' you may have.
- What foundation garments am I going to wear with this dress?
- How am I going to accessorize it?

When you have answered all these questions, you are pretty much there. Make up another toile, incorporating these changes, and look at it again.

Remember that every time you make a toile, you are practising your sewing skills.

Any construction problems that you may encounter will be sorted out on cheap calico. When you've found your perfect dress, it can be made again and again out of lots of different fabrics. It's well worth the time and effort it takes to get your dress just right.

Choosing your Fabric

The choice of fabrics in stores and markets nowadays is dazzling and may be confusing, but a gown that is designed and made well can easily be spoiled if you choose the wrong fabric.

Check out your local fabric shop and ask for advice. Buy a small amount first and sew a few seams to see if it is easy to make up and whether it frays. There are a few key questions you should ask yourself to help you to make the right choice.

- What colour?
- Shiny or matt?
- Heavy or light?
- Natural or man-made?

The rule to remember is that if you use cheap fabric, you get a cheap-looking garment! I tend to stick to just a few fabrics for my gowns, and my favourites include:

Silk dupion

Silk dupion and dupioni are available in hundreds of colours. A distinctive slub in the weave gives the fabric a raw, hand-woven quality. It is quite stiff and lends itself well to structured gowns and bodices. The fabric has a slight sheen but it is not too shiny, and it is easy to work with. It does tend to fray badly so you will need to finish your seams off well.

Two main types are available: hand-woven Indian dupion that is very 'slubby' and the machine-made China version which is much smoother and woven slightly more tightly. The price is about the same, so look at both to decide which would work best. You may find what you want on the internet, where suppliers may offer a discount for larger quantities.

Duchess satin

This beautiful fabric is stiff with lots of body and a distinctive, very shiny surface on one side. It comes in lots of colours but looks best in white, ivory or pastel tones. It frays very badly so can be a little difficult to work with; the fine surface threads may also pull and catch on rough surfaces or even rough hands, and pins may leave marks. But it is a beautiful fabric when made up and is well worth the trouble. It comes in silk and silk mix varieties, as well as man-made duchess which is so good these days that the choice tends to be financial. There really isn't a huge difference in the overall effect.

BEADED LACE: **1**
SILK DUPION: **2** **4** **5**
SILK TAFFETA: **3**
SILK CREPE DE CHINE: **6**
SILK CHARMEUSE: **7**
SATIN-BACKED CREPE: **8**

Taffeta

Taffeta is a much stiffer, crisper and slightly matt fabric that comes in silk and man-made varieties. The fabric comes in plain colours but you can also get 'shot' fabric, which is when the warp and weft threads are of different colours giving a two-tone effect. This is very effective when used in vibrant colours such as purple shot with orange or cerise shot with turquoise.

You can also buy 'water marked' or moiré taffeta. This is where a 'wave' pattern is woven into the fabric. A bit old-fashioned at the moment, but these things have a habit of coming back to haunt us!

Satin backed crepe or charmeuse

This very dense fabric has a matt crepe feel on one side and a shiny satin finish on the other. Either side may be used as the right side: it works well using the matt side for the main dress and the shiny side for trim and bindings. Its soft waterfall effect works well when cut on the bias. It can be quite difficult to handle as it may slip when cutting or sewing, but it's well worth the effort if you want a less structured gown.

Brocade

The pattern is made during the weaving process of this very heavy fabric. It is often used for furnishings, but do not let that put you off: its dense structure and absence of stretch across the straight grain works wonderfully for corsets and basque tops. It may be a bit heavy to use as an all-over fabric, so try it for just the bodice or for an evening jacket. It is available in silk, which is very expensive, or man-made versions.

Lace

There are many different types of lace and you really do get exactly what you pay for. Buy small pieces of lace and experiment to get the look you want. Choose the most expensive lace you can afford as cheap lace looks just that: cheap.

Some lace is actually embroidery on fine net. This looks good used as an overlay, when the main fabric and the lace are sewn together as though one fabric. All-over lace has a border on each side, which can be cut away and used to edge hems and necklines. Guipure lace is expensive, but can look beautiful used sparingly as single motifs, either alone or mixed with all-over lace.

Crepe

Whether in pure silk or man made, crepe clings to the body and drapes wonderfully. Crepe works well cut on both the straight and the bias grain. Take care, as it may also reveal lumps and bumps. Bold, printed crepes flatter any figure type.

Chiffon/georgette

These fine, floaty and sheer fabrics are beautiful to look at and wear but very difficult to sew. They are fine used in small amounts for drapes and embellishments, but for a beginner they are best avoided (oh, I do sound negative!).

If you are a more advanced stitcher and you really want to use chiffon or georgette, give yourself lots of time. Take great care when cutting out, as they tend to slip 'off grain' very easily. Pins will leave marks and the edges will fray very badly. You must set the tension on your machine to perfection, or your seams will pull and pucker. Sew seams slowly, and, if they still pull or pucker, try inserting tissue paper between the layers of fabric before sewing. The tissue will rip out easily after sewing, and is well worth trying, especially on long seams. For the hem, a simple overcast works best.

Organza/organdie

These fabrics are sheer, but are much stiffer and have more 'body' than chiffon so are easier to work with. They work well for blouses and sheer sleeves, and also layered up on full skirts. I once used twenty layers on a full circle ball-gown – imagine sewing the hems on that lot! If you are going to layer, try graduating the colours from dark up to light on the top for stunning effect.

Organza comes in matt, shiny and crystal finishes. I prefer matt, as the others can look a bit 'stagey'. Check out your local fabric shop to see which you prefer.

HOW MUCH FABRIC WILL I NEED?

The amount of fabric you will need for your party dress depends on so many things, including the style of the dress, your size and height, and the chosen fabric. One important rule to remember is always to buy more than you think you will need.

The best way to work out how much fabric you need is to do a 'lay'; literally, lay out the pattern pieces on a length of fabric. Use fabric the same width as you plan to use for your project. Measure carefully, then add at least 20% to allow for adjustments or error. If you want to edge your dress with bias strips, allow for this too. Now round up to the nearest half-yard (50cm).

Most of the dresses in the book are cut on the fold, so a handy tip is to use a length of scrap fabric cut to *half* the width of your chosen fabric – I often use an old sheet. Make sure your grain lines run in the same direction and are parallel to the fold. Lay out the toile pieces, using one edge of the fabric as if it were a fold. Proceed as above. Repeat to calculate the lining.

Embellishments

There are hundreds of ways to embellish your gown. Here are some of my favourites, but don't restrict yourself. Check out your local haberdashery shop, or use your ingenuity – I have bought beaded dresses from charity shops just for the embellishments. I sometimes embroider pieces before sewing them together.

SEQUINS

Don't use too many sequins or you will look like a cabaret act! Same-colour sequins can make a simple dress fit for a princess. Mother-of-pearl cup sequins are wonderful when used to pick out the pattern of lace.

Big hoop sequins

Use these to cover large areas quickly, or scatter randomly round a neckline or hem. Attach by overstitching through the small hole and the fabric at the same time. Never carry threads across the back: if one breaks, you will lose a whole string.

BEADING

Hand beading can look fabulous, but take care – it is easy to overdo it. Try different beading patterns, so you know how long it will take, and how many beads you will need. For lace, or fabrics with woven or printed patterns, pick out details on the bodice or just round the neckline and hem.

String beads

Use these for large designs, working a small area at a time, and joining new beads where you left off.

Bead drops

I love drops and beads. They may be made in any length, and shimmer when the wearer moves.

CRYSTALS

A few crystals can transform a plain gown into something special. They are available to sew on, in a claw setting or as hot-melt crystals, which are applied with a tool that resembles a soldering iron.

These come in lots of sizes, but smaller ones tend to look best. For a stunning effect, try mixing sizes randomly on a hem, or round a neckline. Test on a small piece of your main fabric to make sure that the heat of the tool doesn't melt or burn it.

Hot-melt flat pearls and beads are also available. Ask your local haberdashery shop what is available.

EMBROIDERY

There are many different types of embroidery, so do some research and see which you like the best. A little machine embroidery can look spectacular on a bodice front or the hem of a train. Hand embroidery is a discipline in itself, but feel free to use it if it appeals to you.

Useful Tip

You can buy fabrics ready embellished. This costs more but is worth it if you don't have the time or the ability to do it yourself.

Fabric Flowers

A corsage over one shoulder or a few rosebuds at the hip can look stunning, and are surprisingly easy to make. Use the same fabric as the gown for a subtle approach, or contrasting tones for impact. Chiffon and organza flowers add a more delicate look.

Simple fabric roses

Use strips of fabric. Mine was 18 inches (45cm) long and 4 inches (10cm) wide.

1 Fold the strip in half widthways and finish the long edge. Fold the unfinished edge down to the overlocked edge (**1a**). Stitch along the overlocked edge, gathering as you go (**1b**). Near the end of the seam, fold in the other raw edge, then sew to the end (**1c**).

1a

1b

1c

FABRIC ROSE AND ROSEBUD

2a

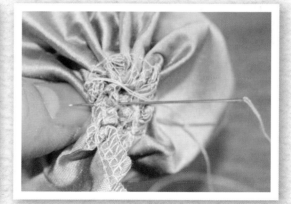

2b

2 Thread a needle with double thread. Starting from one end roll up the fabric, overlocking at the bottom, and stitch in place as you go. You have a rose! (**2a–c**)

2c

Rosebud
Use a shorter and narrower piece of fabric than for the rose.

3 Overlock the fabric and fold over the ends (**3a**). Gather up the strip, less tightly than for the rose (**3b**).

4 Roll up and finish in exactly the same way as for the rose.

3a

3b

4

Peony

Start with a fabric strip slightly wider and longer than for the rose – mine was 22 inches (56cm) by 5 inches (13cm).

1 Overlock and fold in the ends.

2 Roll and secure the 'heart' of the flower (**2a**), then make the first petal shape by twisting the fabric strip round a full 360 degrees (**2b**).

FABRIC PEONY

3 Stitch the base another two thirds of the way round and twist again. Carry on to the end, twisting new petals in as you go (**3a & 3b**).

3a

3b

Making a corsage
Make flowers in any fabric you like and gather them in groups for an elegant corsage. Add some flowers in chiffon or organza to make it extra special.

CORSAGE WITH ORGANZA ROSES

Midnight

This dress is stunning yet easy to create.
The techniques used to make it are extremely valuable,
so you should make at least one.

Midnight

It may surprise you to learn that this dress is just the basic body block with a few subtle adjustments. The version shown is in a purple-blue, satin-backed silk crepe, but it may be made in almost any fabric that drapes well and has some weight. For a crisper look, choose a silk dupion or similar.

Remember the half body block you made for the basque? You're going to use it again. If you're ready, let's make a start.

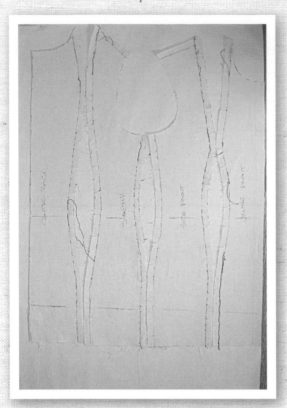

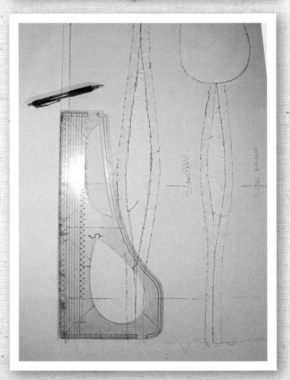

Making the Toile

1 Lay out the body block, centre front to the fold of calico that is long enough for a full-length dress. My pattern pieces fit together with no gaps, but yours may not. There is nothing wrong with this: every body shape is different, so every pattern will look different!

2 Make sure the waist lines are at 90° to the fold so they lie on the straight grain (**2a**). Draw round the pattern pieces. Add a ⅝ inch (1.5cm) seam allowance to the centre back (**2b**).

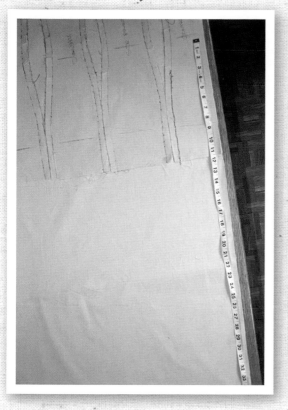

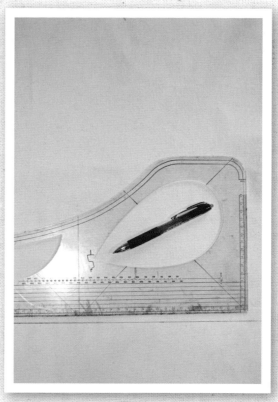

4a

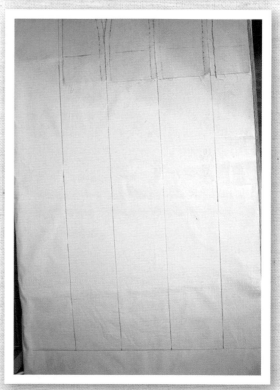

4b

3 Wearing heels the same height as you plan to wear with your dress, measure from waist to floor. Mark this length down the centre-front line from the waist line on your body block (the fold of the fabric) and add ⅜ inch (1cm).

4 Using your set square, draw in the hem line at right angles to the folded edge, through the mark and right across the width of the fabric (**4a**). Draw lines down from all vertical seams to the hem line, using the set square and a long straight edge so they run at right angles (**4b**).

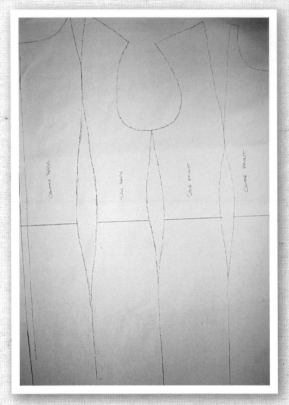

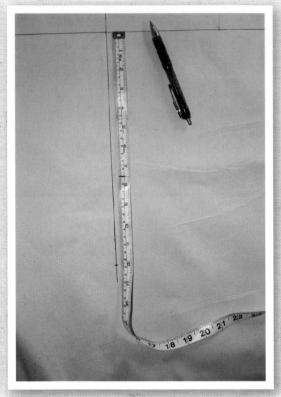

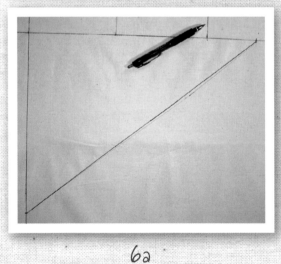

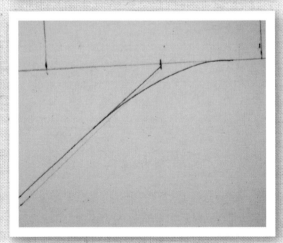

6a

6b

5 Mark in the waist lines from the body block and name the pattern pieces (**5a**). Extend the centre-back line down past the hem line, and mark in the required train length – 12 inches (30cm) in this case (**5b**).

6 Make a mark at the hem line, about halfway along the side front piece, and join to the train length mark (**6a**). Round off the front hem edge using the curves on your designer's set square (**6b**).

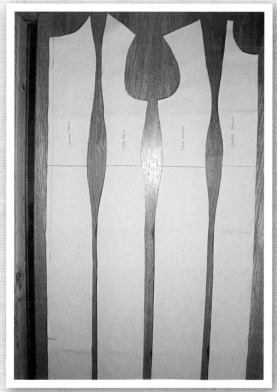

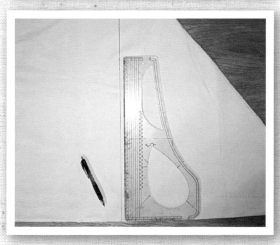

8

7 Extend the seam lines down to the new hem line (**7a**). Cut out pattern pieces (**7b**).

8 Square off the calico at 90 degrees to the fold using the set square. Decide where you want the train to begin to flare out – just below the knee is ideal. Measure this distance up from the floor for the godet length – in this case 30 inches (75cm). Add the train length.

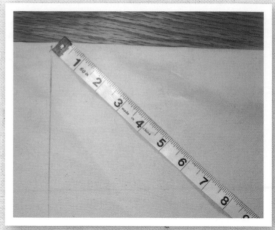

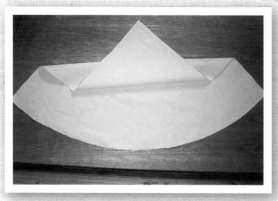

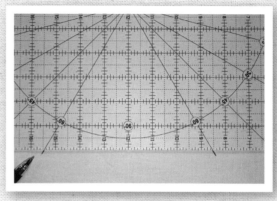

10a 10b

9 Place the end of the tape measure at the point you squared off and measure out the godet length (**9a**). Keeping one end steady and moving the other in an arc, mark in the godet length at regular intervals (**9b**).

10 Cut out on the lines and open out the semi-circle. Using a ruler marked with angles, place the 90-degree mark on the fold and make a mark at the two 60-degree points (**10a & 10b**).

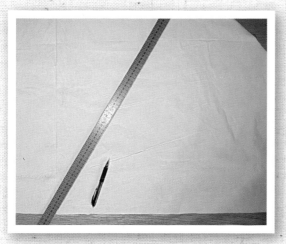

12a

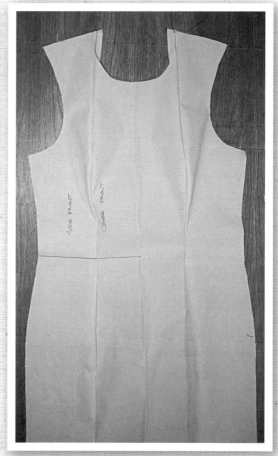

11 Remove the ruler and join the centre
fold line at the straight edge, through the
marks, to divide the semi-circle into three
equal parts (**11a**). Cut out on the lines (**11b**).

12 Now all the pieces are cut out, join the
side-front and centre-front pieces as for the
body block (**12a**). The waist lines you drew
in should match; if not, undo the seam and
try again. Sew the other side-front seam to
complete the front of the toile (**12b**).

12b

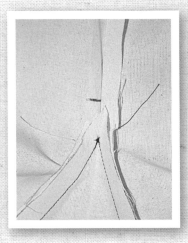

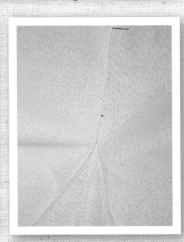

14   15a   15b

13 Take one centre-back piece and the centre godet, right sides together. With the round edge of the godet at the hem edge and the point facing up the back seam, join using a ⅝ inch (1.5cm) seam. When the needle reaches the fold line, stop and backstitch. The fabric is marked to show where the stitching stops (**13a & 13b**).

14 Join the second centre-back piece to the first, right sides together. Start stitching about 8 inches (20cm) down from the top towards the hem, where the zip will go on the actual dress. Stop stitching exactly where the stitching on the godet begins.

15 Open up the godet so its other seam line runs down the centre-back seam, and, starting exactly where that stitching ends, finish off the seam. It should lie beautifully in the centre-back seam (**15a & 15b**).

16 Repeat for the second and third godets in the side-back seams, sewing them in just as for the centre-back seam. Add the godets first, keeping the stitching lines accurate, then the side-back pieces, stitching from the top towards the hem (**16a**). The back toile is now finished (**16b**).

17 Fold the back in half along the centre-back seam and mark in the new hem line, smoothing the curves as you go (**17a**). Cut out on the lines (**17b**).

17b

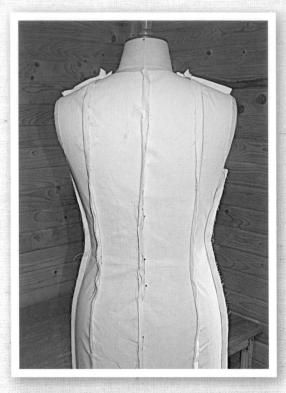

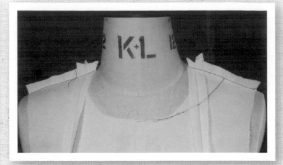

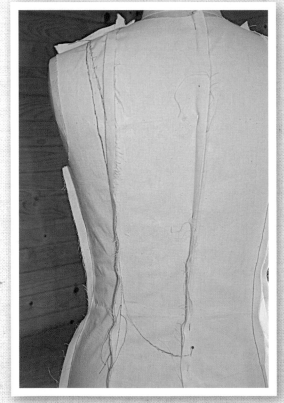

18 Join the front and back, sewing the side, then the shoulder seams. Try on the toile: there should be no need to alter it. If there is, you may want to go back and re-do the body block. Mark in the new front neckline (**18a & 18b**).

19 Draw in the back neck shape. The back opening has been dropped below the waist line. Remember, if you do this you will not be able to wear any foundation garments (**19a**). Check that the hem line is smooth and that the train is not too long (**19b**).

The Dress

20 Undo the toile, fold the centre-front piece in half and press. You will need one centre-back, one side-back, one side-front and the centre-front piece folded in half, plus all three godet pieces. Lay out the pieces on your main fabric, checking that they are on the straight grain (**20a & 20b**).

21 Cut out the pieces (**21a**). Cut 1½ inch (4cm) bias strips for the neck and armholes, as in the techniques section (**21b**).

22 Overlock or overcast all the seams to prevent fraying. Sew the side-fronts to the centre front just as for the toile (**22a**). Snip into the curved seams to just before the stitching line (**22b**).

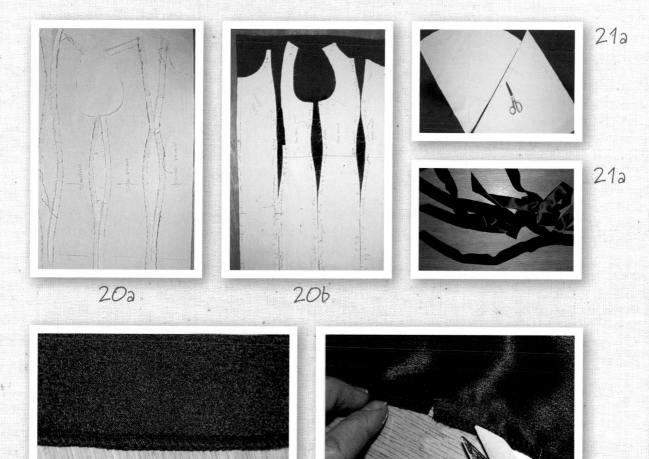

20a

20b

21a

21a

22a

22b

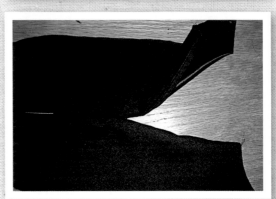

23 Complete the front, pressing the seams open as you go (**23a**). Add the centre godet to the centre-back seam (**23b**).

24 Insert a concealed zip, 8 inches (20 cm) or the length you need to come to your hip line, in the centre-back seam (**24a**). Finish the back seam, trapping in the godet as before (**24b**).

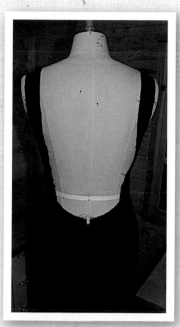

25 Complete the back as for the toile. Sew the side and shoulder seams, then try on your dress to check the fit (**25a–c**).

26 Bias bind the neck opening and armholes, folding in the edges as for the binding on the basic basque (see page 82) and stitching at ⅜ inch (1cm). The shiny side of the bias has been used as the right side (**26a & 26b**).

26a

26b

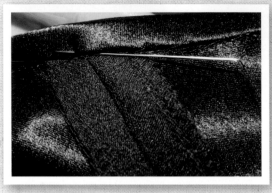
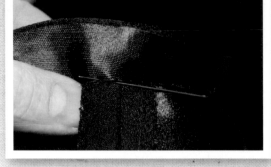

28b 28c

27 Fold in the edges and pin them in place at the side seam of the armhole opening (**27a**). Stitch at ⅜ inch (1cm) as for the neck binding (**27b**).

28 Using satin bias binding, bias bag the hem as in the basic techniques section (see page 38). Sew the bindings and hem in place by hand (**28a–28c**).

29 Sew a hook and eye to the top opening of the zip, press the dress well and it will be ready to wear.

Variation

All I have done here is crop the gown at thigh level and cover it in large sequins – it took me a week to sew them on!

Vintage

I love this dress. It conjures up visions of 1950s Hollywood,
but it is really easy to make. If you don't tell anyone,
I promise I won't!

Vintage

I've used a stiff silk dupion in a fabulous fuchsia, but you could make this dress in any 'stand out in the crowd' shade. Make the skirt as long and elegant or as short and flirty as you like, the techniques are the same. Layer more underskirts and wear it with killer heels and fishnet stockings for even more of a *Sex and the City* look.

Remember the basic basque? This dress is just an extension of it, but with a zip instead of lacing. You can even use the same pattern.

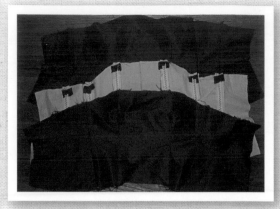

1a

1b

2

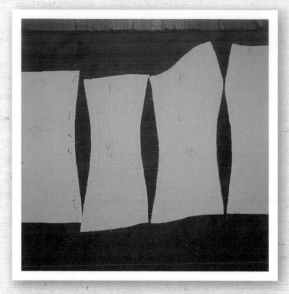

3

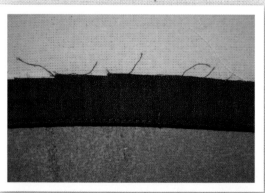

1 Lay out the pattern pieces exactly as for the basque (see page 79). Add a ⅝ inch (1.5cm) allowance to the centre-back seam for the zip as you will not be using lacing. Cut out in main fabric, in calico and again for lining – in this version the same fabric is used for top and lining. Make up the three sections as for the basque, boning the calico interlining (**1a & 1b**).

2 Place the lining and calico interlining wrong sides together, and stitch a ⅝ inch (1.5cm) seam down both centre-back edges.

3 Fold these edges towards the calico insert. Press a ⅝ inch (1.5cm) fold so the stitching line just shows on the wrong side.

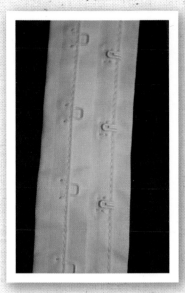

4 The dress will fit very tightly, so add strong hook-and-eye fastener tape (from good haberdashery stores) to the lining to reduce the strain on the zip. White is shown, but you may prefer to match your fabric. Cut the tape about 2 inches (5cm) shorter than the centre-back seam. Measure down the centre back beginning 1 inch (2.5cm) from the top, and mark with a pin. (**4a**). Bring the sides together to check the placement (**4b**).

5 With the right side of the fabric up, lay the eye side on the left of the centre-back seam. Line up the top eye with the pin, and the edge of the eyes with the edge of the fabric. Sew down the tape using the zipper foot, taking care not to break the needle when you reach the eyes (**5a & 5b**).

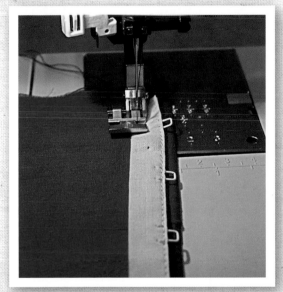

5b

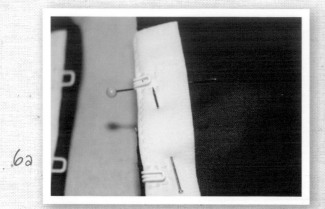

6a

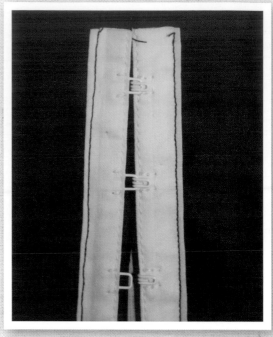

6b

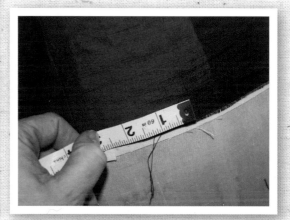

7a

7b

6 Repeat for the hook side. When the tape is fastened the top and bottom of the basque should be perfectly level, and the folded-in edges at the centre back should just meet (**6a & 6b**).

7 Try on the top to make sure all is well (**7a**). Measure round the bottom edge and note this measurement (**7b**).

8 Now for some maths! Divide the bottom edge measurement by 3.142 (trust me!) and halve the result. This 'radius' measurement will be used to curve the top of the skirt so it fits the bottom of the basque exactly. The skirt uses the full width of the fabric so there is little waste.

Measure the width of the fabric, double it, and use this measurement to cut two lengths of fabric for the skirt. Fold each in half to make a perfect square and place the squares, folded edges together, on your cutting table or the floor. Take the folded edge to the selvedge to form a triangle.

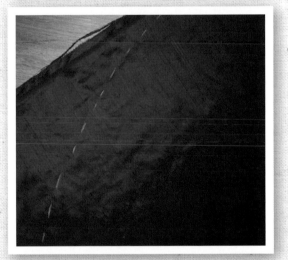

9 Now draw a quarter-circle on the fabric (**9a**). Grab the far corner of the top layer of the fabric at the folded edge. Move this corner carefully round towards the folded edge, marking its progress across the fabric beneath and holding the corner nearest you in place. This sounds complicated, but try it – you are effectively using the edge of the fabric like a pair of compasses. Cut out on the marked line (**9b**).

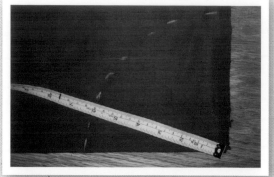

10a

10 Mark out the radius measurement (see step 8) as a quarter of a curve on the point edge of the skirt (**10a**), and cut out on the line (**10b**). You do not need to add a seam allowance to this measurement because the two side seams compensate for it. I can't explain why this works, but it does!

10b

11 Open up the fabric into two half circles and place right sides together. Sew the seams down the selvedges on both sides and press open. Now fold the skirt in half the other way so the seams touch and line up. Place a pin about 6 inches (15cm) down from the waist on one fold line, and cut down this line for the zip opening.

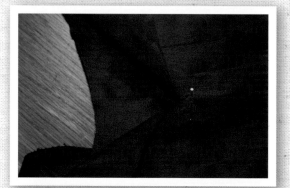

11

12 Cut two bias strips 7 inches (17.5cm) wide across the width of the fabric for the hip bands. Fold them in half widthways, and square up the ends.

Useful Tip

For a shorter skirt, work out your desired skirt length and add ⅜ inch (1cm) for the hem. Add the radius measurement (see step 8). Double the total, then measure down the selvedge of your fabric. Cut across the full width of the fabric. Repeat so you have two rectangles of fabric.

12

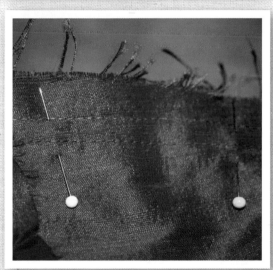

14a 14b

13 Take the main fabric basque and lay on the folded hip band, right sides and raw edges together and lining up the hip seam (**13a**). Pin in place, leaving an overhang of about 2 inches (5cm) at each edge. Sew down using a ⅜ inch (1cm) seam allowance (**13b**).

14 Right sides together, pin the skirt waist seam to the bottom edge of the basque. Line up the zip slash in the back of the skirt with the centre-back seams and trap the hip sash between the layers (**14a**). This should fit exactly, but if not, take a tiny tuck; no-one will notice. Stitch using a ⅜ inch (1.5cm) seam allowance (**14b**).

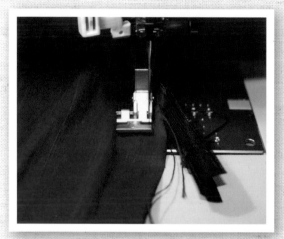

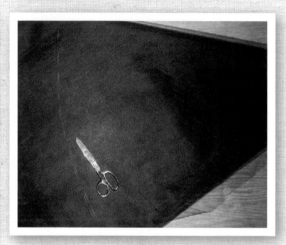

15 Measure from the top of the basque to the bottom of the zip slash in the skirt, then measure down the same distance from the top of a concealed zip in a coordinating colour. At this point, sew several times over the teeth of the zip by hand or machine. Cut off the zip about 1 inch (2.5cm) below this stitching.

16 Insert the zip as in the basic techniques section (see page 43). Make sure the hip sash is folded towards the hem. Stitch the zip through it and the skirt, ending level with the end of the skirt opening slash.

Continue for about 3 inches (7.5cm) down the seam after inserting the zip – there is no need to seam right down to the skirt hem. Backstitch to secure (**16a & 16b**).

17 Cut out several full circle skirts in dress net as for the main fabric. The more layers, the fuller the effect. I used four, which took 20 yards of net! Join the side seams of each underskirt, place all the layers together and stitch round the waist using a ⅜ inch (1cm) seam to hold them together. Slash down through the layers of net, just as for the zip opening of the top skirt.

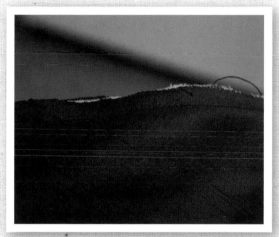

19a

19b

18 Stitch a line ⅜ inch (1 cm) down from the top of the basque lining to hold the two layers together (**18a**). Do the same at the bottom (**18b**).

19 Stitch the net underskirts to the bodice using a ⅝ inch (1.5cm) seam (**19a**). Place the lining inside the main dress and stitch round the top of the basque at ⅝ inch (1.5cm) to hold the layers together (**19b**).

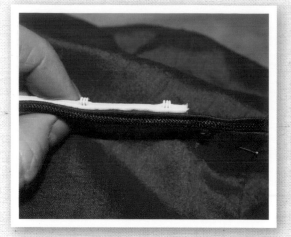

21a

21b

20 Align the fabric edge of the lining with the fabric edge of the main dress and pin in place (**20a & 20b**).

21 Fold back the lining slightly and sew the zip tape to the lining by hand, making sure that the stitches do not show on the right side of the dress (**21a**). Stitch a little way in from the edge, or the zip will not do up. Repeat for the other side (**21b**).

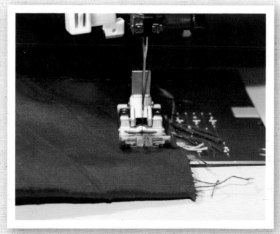

23a 23b 23c

22 Take the second bias band (see step 12) with the raw edges together. Working on the *lining* side of the dress, place the band on the top edge of the basque, folding about 2 inches (5cm) or so to the right side. Sew the top seam using a ⅝ inch (1.5cm) seam allowance. Stop and trim the end to 2 inches (5cm) and turn this under before you finish the seam (**22a & 22b**).

23 Pull up the top band and fold the corner of the band in on both sides to mitre it (**23a**). Catch in place by hand, making sure that none of the stitches show on the right side (**23b & 23c**). See how fabulous the inside of your dress looks!

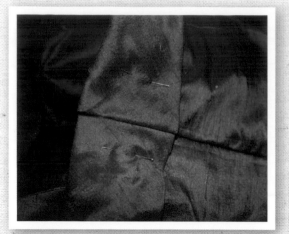

25

24 Fold the band down to the right side. Pin in place at the back seam, making sure that both sides match (**24a**). Fold back the corners and stitch into place (**24b**).

25 Using satin bias binding as shown or bias strips cut from the main fabric, bias bag the hem. Machine stitch the binding to the hem edge, and finish off the inside by hand. This will take a long time (the dress shown took three hours) but is well worth the effort for a perfect finish.

Trimming Your Dress

The top sash of your dress folds down, and the hip sash folds up at the front, then down at the back where it tucks into the zip seam. This gives a really nice line where the skirt joins the bodice.

I've added a padded fabric bow to the sashes, but you could leave it plain or add fabric flowers instead. The choice is yours!

Making a Bow

26 Cut two rectangles of fabric, twice the length and twice the width of your desired bow. Fold the short edges into the centre and seam top and bottom (**26a & 26b**).

27 Turn through to the right side, pushing out the corners to make them nice and square. Cut a couple of layers of stiff net the same size as your bow and stuff them inside (**27a & 27b**).

28 Sew the opening closed. Cut out a small rectangle of fabric about 2 inches (5cm) by 3 inches (7.5cm) (**28a & 28b**)

26a

26b

27a

27b

28a

28b

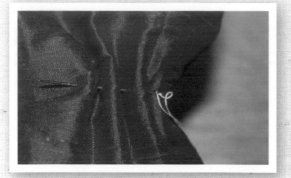

29a

29b

30a

30b

29 Run a gathering stitch through the centre of your bow, draw up and fasten off. Take the rectangle of fabric and fold it into three across the width (**29a & 29b**).

30 Wrap this round the gathered-up bow and stitch the raw edges at the back. Make another bow in the same way (**30a & 30b**).

31 Attach bows neatly to the top and bottom right-hand bust seams. Now you're ready to dance the night away!

31

Variation

Here, the skirt length is shorter, but I made up two full circle skirts and sewed them on together. The top skirt was then pulled up at the front and held in place with a hand-made flower.

Elegance

This halter-neck dress flatters most figure shapes and the stunning print makes it really stand out from the crowd. Use any soft fabric with a good drape.

Elegance

The dress is much easier to construct than it looks, so I have incorporated some extras to learn along the way: making a paper pattern, using darts, and inserting a zip in the side seam. The first ten steps show the creation of the paper pattern, and the instructions for making the dress begin at step 11.

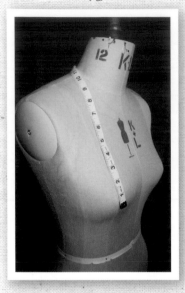

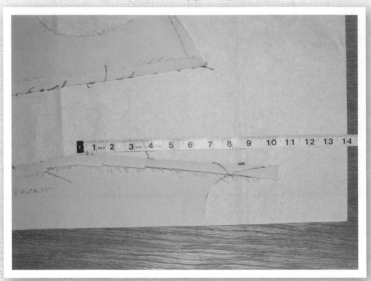

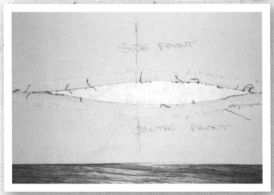

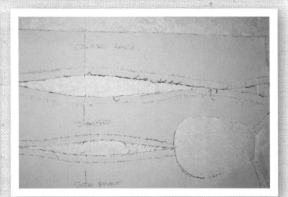

Making the Paper Pattern

1 Lay out a large sheet of paper – brown paper is fine. Measure from your bust point to your centre-back neck and mark this measurement in from the right-hand edge of the paper (**1a**). Take the body block with the seam allowances on, fold in the bust and centre-back seams and press on the stitching line. Place the centre-front bust point to the mark on the paper (**1b**).

2 Place the remaining body block pieces so the lines at the waist run at right angles to the edge of the paper and the bust and hip points join (**2a**). If your figure is top- or bottom-heavy they won't join, but don't worry – you can just run seams from top to bottom as for Midnight (see page 104). Draw in the side seams, under the armhole, the centre-back line (don't add a seam allowance) and the diamond-shaped gaps in the bust and centre back seams (**2b**).

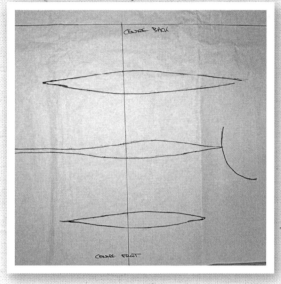

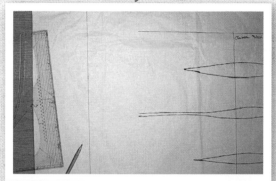

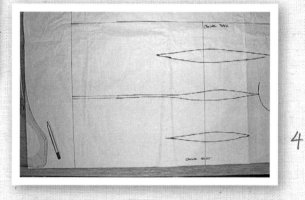

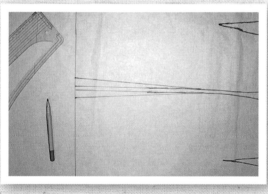

4

3 Remove the body block pieces and mark in the waist line (**3a**). Measure from your waist to thigh level. Mark this measurement plus ⅜ inch (1cm) on the pattern, measuring down from the waist line. Draw in the hem line at right angles to the centre-front edge of the paper (**3b**).

4 Extend the side seam and centre-back seam lines down to the hem line and at right angles to it. Mark the centre front and centre back on your pattern.

5 To taper the dress slightly at thigh level, mark in about ⅜ inch (1cm) from the side seams (**5a**). Join up these points from the fullest part of the hips. Scribble out the unwanted lines to prevent confusion when cutting out (**5b**).

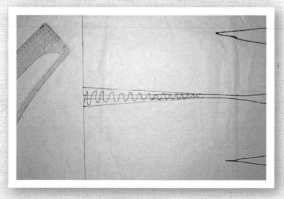

5a

5b

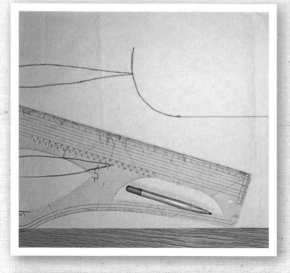

6a

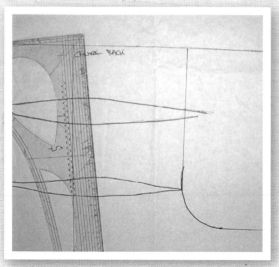

6b

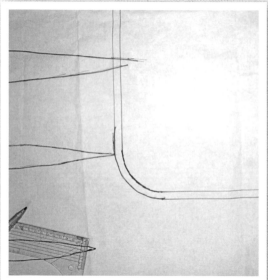

7a

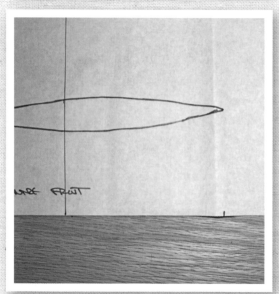

7b

6 Using the designer's set square, strike a line at right angles from the right edge of your paper to the inside edge of the armhole line (**6a**). Draw in a line, at a right angle to the centre-back line, to the underarm curve. Add a ⅜ inch (1cm) seam allowance to this line (**6b**).

7 Mark the centre-front edge of your pattern where you want the lowest part of the V-neck to come. Use the bust point mark as a reference point (**7a & 7b**).

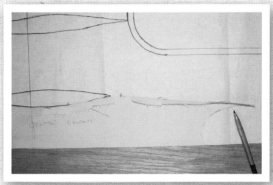

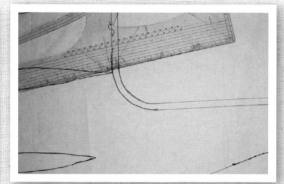

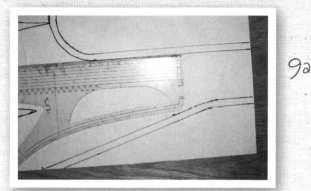

8 Place the centre-front block piece back on the pattern, lining up the waist line, and mark at the widest part of the neck (**8a**). Remove the block piece. Join this mark and the V mark, then curve the line so that it is at right angles to the right hand edge of the paper. Add a ⅜ inch (1cm) seam allowance to this edge (**8b**).

9 Add a ⅜ inch (1cm) seam allowance to the neck edge (**9a**), and cut out the pattern pieces (**9b**).

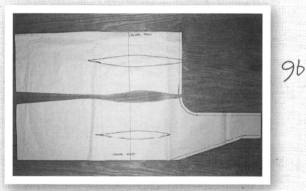

10 Mark in a ⅜ inch (1cm) hem line, then mark this line ⅝ inch (1.5cm) in from the side seams. Measure in from the centre back and the centre front to this mark. Add up these measurements to obtain the 'hemline measurement'. I often write this on the pattern.

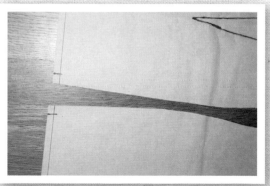

Making the Dress

11 Place the centre-front and centre-back lines on the fold of the fabric as the zip will be in the side seam. Pin the pattern pieces carefully on the fabric, making sure it stays on the straight grain (**11a**). Cut out (**11b**).

12 Repeat with the lining fabric. I've used pure silk, but synthetic lining may be substituted if it is about the same weight as the main fabric.

13 Mark in the darts. Each piece can be marked separately from the pattern, but it is easier to push a pin through the points of the darts and through their widest part, as shown – which may not be at the waist line (**13a & 13b**).

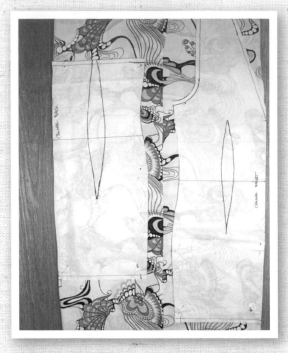

11a

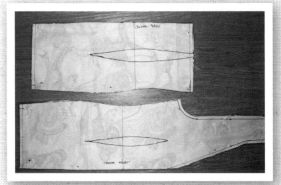

11b

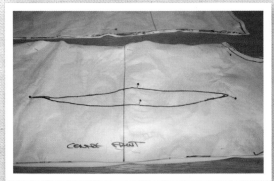

12

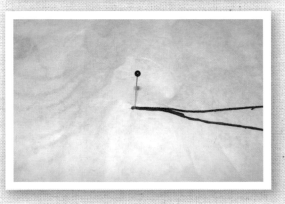

13a

13b

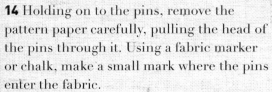

14 Holding on to the pins, remove the pattern paper carefully, pulling the head of the pins through it. Using a fabric marker or chalk, make a small mark where the pins enter the fabric.

15 Leaving the pins in place, pull the top fabric out of the way slightly, and mark where the pins go through the fabric again. You will be marking both the top and the lining fabric.

16 Flip the fabrics over and mark where the pins come through the other side (**16a**). Repeat for the back, snipping inside the seam allowance to mark where the dart runs off the top (**16b**).

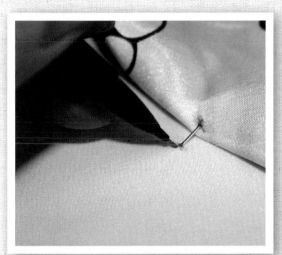

15

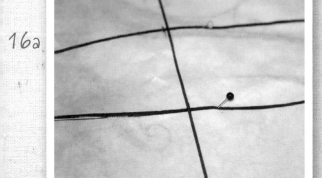

16a

16b

18a

18b

17 Lay out the main fabric and lining, right sides together, and stitch round the armholes using a ⅜ inch (1cm) seam allowance, Snip into the curved parts of the fabric at about 1 inch (2.5cm) intervals, stopping just before the stitching line.

18 Stitch the neckline, using the same seam allowance. Stop at the V-point with the needle down in the fabric, then lift the presser foot, turn, and stitch up the other side of the neck (**18a**). Snip into the curves and down to just before the stitching line at the V-point (**18b**).

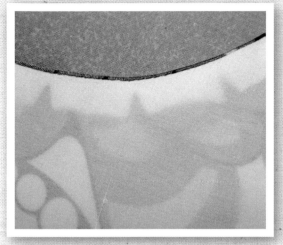

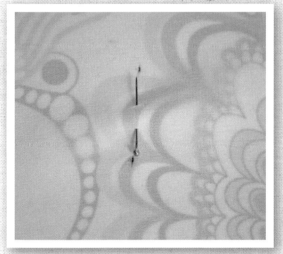

20a

19 Turn everything through to the right side and press on the wrong side, allowing just a tiny bit of the main fabric to show (**19a & 19b**).

20 For the darts, place a pin between the mid dart points (**20a**) and at each end point to hold the fabric layers together (**20b**).

20b

21a

21b

22

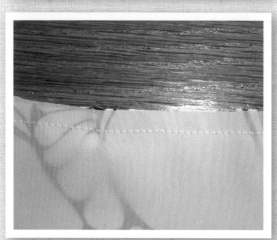

23

21 Fold the fabric in half, from end point to end point, making sure that the mid-point marks match up, and stitch from the mid-point mark to the end, running the stitching off as in the techniques section (see page 30). Turn over, and finish the dart (**21a & 21b**).

22 Press towards the side seam, and repeat for the second dart. Overlock or overcast the side seams through both layers of fabric

23 Right sides together, sew across the top of the back pieces using a ⅜ inch (1cm) seam allowance.

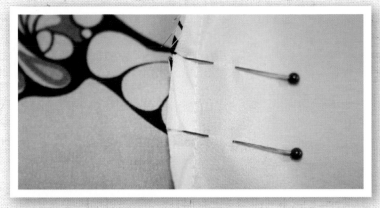

24a

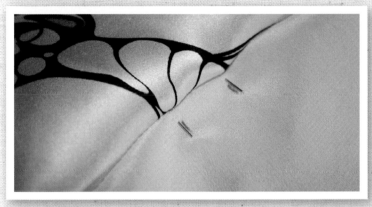

24b

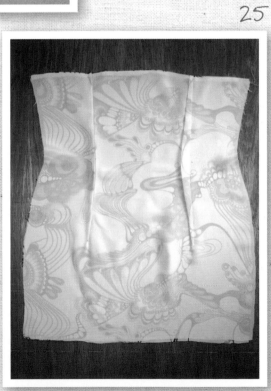

25

24 Push pins through the lining fabric by the snips marking the top of the dart (**24a**), and mark the right side of the lining (**24b**).

25 Complete the darts as for the front, running off the top of the darts at the marks. Press towards the centre back. Overlock or overcast the side seams.

26a

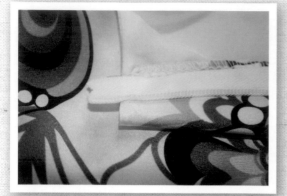

26b

26 To place the concealed zip in the left side seam, start with the little 'stop' of the zip tape level with the top of the dress at the underarm (**26a**). Stitch in the zip as normal, but this time follow the curve of the fabric, keeping the stitching line ⅝ inch (1.5cm) in from the edge. Finish the other side (**26b**).

27 Try on the dress and make any adjustments you feel are required.

27

28 Fold the dress in half, side seam to side seam, and mark the centre folds front and back with pins.

29 Divide the hemline measurement (see step 10) by 3.142 and halve the result to calculate the radius measurement. Use this to cut out a full circle skirt across the full width of the fabric, as for Vintage (see page 125). Sew one seam of the circle and, with right sides together, match it up with the pin at the centre back of the dress. Pin the open seam of the circle to the dress at the centre-front pin, overlapping the seams about ⅝ inch (1.5cm). Finish pinning the circle to the dress. The skirt should join the dress perfectly at thigh level; if not, take tiny tucks at the back.

30 Sew the seam and overlock or overcast it to finish. Try on the dress and pin up the front edges to the required length.

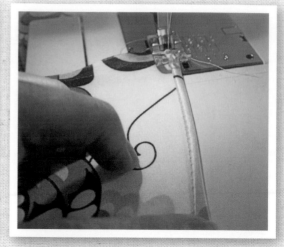

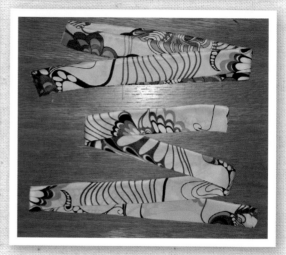

33a

33b

31 Lay out the dress with the circle folded in half along the centre back seam. Cut the hem, running the cut line off to the full length of the circle somewhere around the side seams of the dress. This will give a nice flow to the train.

32 Overlock or overcast the hem to make it easier to turn and help to keep it narrow. Take a double turned up hem over the overcasting (see basic techniques, page 37).

33 Cut two pieces of fabric about 4 inches (10cm) deep across the fabric width for the ties (**33a**). Fold in half, right sides together, and stitch across the narrow end and down the length using a ⅜ inch (1cm) seam. Turn through and press, using a knitting needle to assist (**33b**).

34a

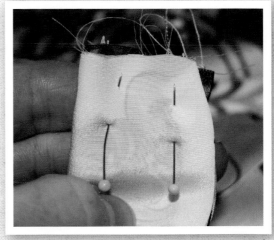

34b

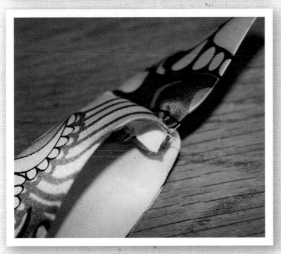

35a

35b

34 At the top edge of the dress where the ties will go, fold the raw edge in half with right sides together, trapping the raw edge of the tie inside (**34a**) and pin (**34b**).

35 Stitch across the raw edge using a ⅝ inch (1.5cm) seam allowance (**35a**). I often stitch this seam twice as it needs to be strong. Turn to the right side and stitch down the open edge about 2 inches (5cm) very near the edge of the fabric (**35b**).

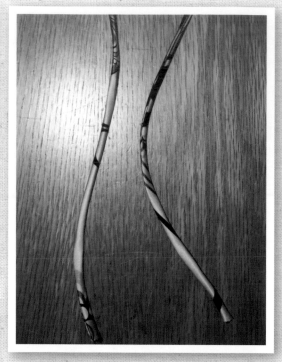

 37b

36 Fold the top of the zip tape inside the seam and hand sew across the top edge.

37 Make two pieces of rouleau, each about 17 inches (43cm) long as in basic techniques (see page 47). Tuck in the ends of the rouleau and stitch (**37a & 37b**).

38 Press your dress and try it on. Tie the rouleau round the halter-neck straps to give a nice shape to the fabric over the bust, and set off for the premiere of the latest blockbuster!

38

Variation

To make the short version, I omitted
the full-circle skirt and replaced
the ties on the shoulder straps with
some fabulous diamanté buckles.
The hem has been bias bagged.

Belle

This is the most spectacular gown, but in many ways it's the easiest to make. The only new skill needed is gathering, but this is easy – you will have no trouble at all.

Belle

My gown is lemon-yellow with a black trim and underlay, but any 'show stopper' colour can be used – scarlet would be fabulous. My usual motto is 'less is more', but in this case, add as many fabric flowers as you like!

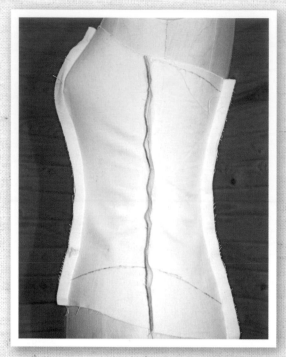

1a

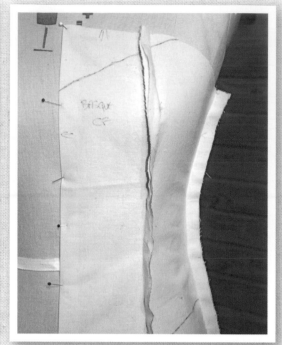

1b

1 Make up a half block of the basque (see page 75) and try it on (**1a**). Mark in new top and bottom lines in any shape you like. The bottom shape shown here echoes the shape of the top, then lifts over the hip and drops back down to the bottom of the basque (**1b**).

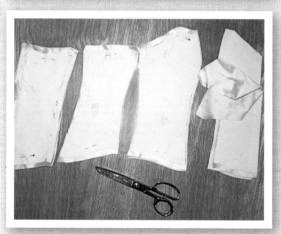

2

2 Unpick the toile and cut on the new top and bottom lines. Cut out the main fabric, lining and calico interlining as for the basque (see page 79), adding ⅝ inch (1.5cm) to the centre-back seam and the bottom of the bodice. As the top will be bagged in rather than bound, add ⅜ inch (1cm) seam allowance to the top of the basque.

3 Make up three separate bodices as for the basque. To avoid catching the boning when bagging in the top seam, mark seams that will be boned, measuring ⅜ inch (1cm) down from the top and ⅝ inch (1.5cm) up from the bottom (**3a & 3b**).

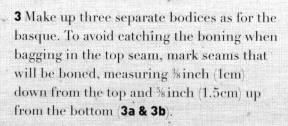

3a   3b

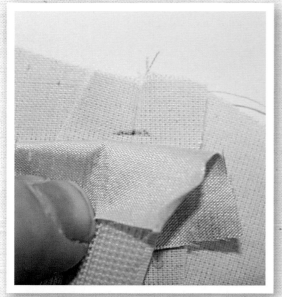

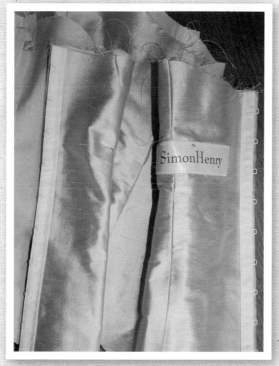

4 Place the bones on the seams, starting just below the top mark and ending just before the bottom mark. Cover the ends of the bones with scrap fabric (**4a & 4b**).

5 Add as many bones as you need for support. In the example, a few extra bones have been added because the top points do not end on a seam line; yours may be different (**5a**). Join the lining and interlining, adding hook-and-eye tape as for Vintage (see page 123). A label may be added to the lining (**5b**).

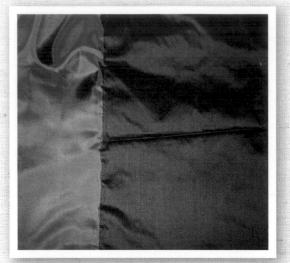

6

Useful Tip

If you do not want to drape the front of your dress you can line the whole skirt with cheaper fabric as it will not show.

7a

7b

6 As the dress front is draped, the part of the skirt lining that shows is made from better-quality fabric. Cut a length of lining fabric about five times your hip measurement, then cut a length of better fabric about twice your hip measurement. With right sides together, making sure the waist edge is straight, join the raw ends of the top fabric and lining to form a big tube. Don't worry if they don't match at the hem at this stage. Finish the raw seam edges.

7 Fold the 'tube' of lining in half with the main fabric panel slightly off to the side you plan to pull up. At the fold that will be the centre back, measure down 6 inches (15cm) and mark with a pin. Cut down the fold line to the pin and finish off the raw edge (**7a & 7b**).

8 Gather the skirt lining to the bodice lining, making sure its right side is on the inside. Place the bodice lining inside the skirt lining with the right side to the outside and the bottom edge pointing upwards – the right sides of the fabrics should be together. Pin the skirt opening to the centre-back seams on both sides.

9 Mark the centre front of the bodice interlining with a pin. Fold the skirt in half to find the centre front and pin to the centre front of the bodice. Fold the lining in half between the centre back and centre front and pin to the side seam at this point. Repeat on the other side (**9a & 9b**).

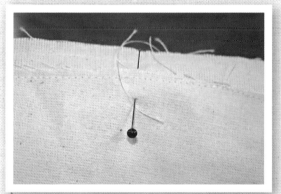

9a

9b

10a

Useful Tip

Net underskirts can be added as for Vintage (see page 128) but you will need 10–15 layers. I have discovered that a ready-made underskirt from a bridal salon is far cheaper – if you prefer to buy one, do so before you start your dress.

10b

10 The skirt lining will now be pinned to the bodice at the centre-front, centre-back and side seams (**10a**). Find the mid-point of these 'pleats' and pin to the bodice here. Repeat two or three times, reducing the size of the pleats by half each time. This sounds more complicated than it is, and you will soon get the hang of it (**10b & 10c**).

10c

12

13

11 With the lining upwards, stitch the seam ⅝ inch (1.5cm) in, gathering the lining with your fingers as you go. You can sew over the pins, but remove each one as you pass it so you do not leave any (**11a & 11b**).

12 The bodice lining and the skirt lining are now attached.

13 Add the main skirt to the main bodice. From the bottom of the back bodice seam, measure the length you want the longest part of the train to be. Fold a length of fabric about six times your hip measurement in half lengthways. Measure along the selvedge and snip in from the raw edges to mark the train length.

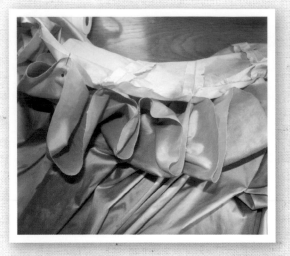

14a

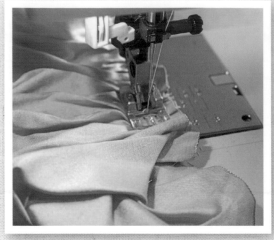

14b

15

16

14 Open out the skirt and pin these snip marks to the centre-back edges of the bottom of the bodice, right sides together. Gather the skirt onto the bodice exactly as for the lining. Do not gather the train length onto the bodice at either end. Sew the seam as for the lining (**14a & 14b**).

15 You will see that the train length is made from the parts of the skirt that are not gathered on to the bodice. At this point, most students say: 'Oh, that's clever!' so I'll wait a moment…

16 Insert a concealed zip in the back seam, going down about 6 inches (15cm) into the train. Make sure the bodice seams match exactly. If not, unpick and do it again!

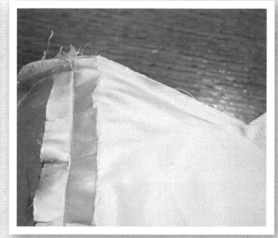

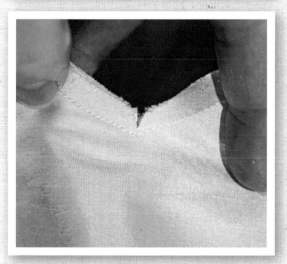

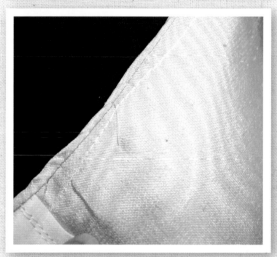

17c 18

17 To attach the lining to the main dress, take the main dress with the right side outside, and the lining with the right side inside. Place the main dress inside the lining so the right sides are together. Pin the lining bodice to the main bodice at the seams (**17a**). Sew across the top of the bodice using a ⅜ inch (1cm) seam and avoiding the tops of the bones (**17b**). Notch the curved parts of the seam and snip into the front 'V' (**17c**).

18 Turn the dress through to the right side. There will be quite a lot of fabric, but take your time and it will be fine. Press the top seam, rolling the lining very slightly to the inside (see Elegance, page 147).

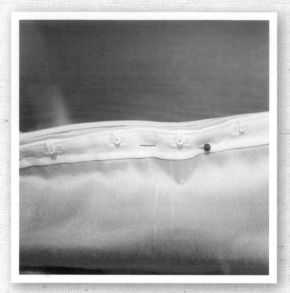

19a

19b

19 Sew the lining to the top as for Vintage (see page 29) **19a & 19b**.

20 That's the main part of the dress done!

20

Embellishing the Dress

Of course, you could leave it there, but this is me, so let's embellish! I'll let you decide how many flowers to add.

21 The flowers that cascade over one shoulder will sit on tabs. To make these, cut two pieces of fabric 3 inches (7.5cm) by 6 inches (15cm) and fold in half lengthways. Seam down the raw side and across the top, then turn through and press. Sew one tab to the front bodice at the angle required to go over the arm.

22 Make strips of fabric for flowers as in the embellishments section (see page 96). Make several lengths of rouleau the full width of your fabric (see page 47).

23 Make the flowers and sew in place by hand, making sure all raw edges are hidden (**23a & 23b**).

21

22

23a

23b

24a

24b

25

26

24 Add some rouleau loops to your corsage (**24a**). Add some rouleau to the end of the tab for tying the arm flowers (**24b**).

25 Add a tab to the back at the angle required to fall over the arm. Add rouleau just as at the front so the flowers can be tied over one arm. Add some flowers to the hip opposite the arm flowers, and take a few round to the back.

Try on the gown over the underskirts. Pin the hem to the required length on both lining and the top fabric, rounding off the points of the train. Double-turn and hem the lining. Bias bind the top dress hem (this took four hours of hand sewing).

26 Pull up one side of the top skirt so the good lining fabric shows, and stitch in place. Prepare yourself for the gasps of admiration when you make your entrance!

Variation

All I have done here is to cut the skirt off at thigh level. Instead of the flower trim, I've added some hot-melt crystals to the bodice.

Acknowledgements

GMC Publications would like to thank

Chris Gloag, and his assistant Guillaume Serve, for the brilliant fashion photography.

Andrea from Zone Models.

Louise Compagnone for styling and inspiration.

AJ for make-up.

Simon Henry for hair.

Doodles the bunny, and Mel for looking after him.

The following companies for allowing us to photograph on their premises, and for all their help:

PAUL CLARK
94 High Street,
Lewes, East Sussex,
BN7 1XH
www.paulclarkclothiers.com

PELHAM HOUSE HOTEL
St. Andrews Lane,
Lewes, East Sussex,
BN7 1UW
www.pelhamhouse.com

The following, for their help with props and accessories:

THE BOOTH MUSEUM, Brighton *for the loan of their flamingo and rook.*

LK BENNETT *for shoes.*

PHILIP PARFITT at Wardrobe (see address below) *for vintage jewellery.*

WARDROBE
51 Upper North Street,
Brighton,
East Sussex,
BN1 3FH
For accessories.

EMMA FOSTER at GMC Publications *for all her help.*

Author's Acknowledgements

A project like this book is by no means a one-man enterprise: though my name is on the front cover, it would not have happened without many other people.Thanks to all at GMC, especially Gerrie, Jonathan P and Jonathan B for finding me, and for giving me the opportunity to share my work and my vision with you. To Virginia, Gilda, Hedda and all the girls. To my fabulous editor, Alison Howard, thank you for keeping 'my voice'. Very special thanks goes to Louise Compagnone (tall sister) for her vision, good taste in styling matters and for just being fabulous. To Pfaff machines, and a special thanks to Derby Cloth House for the best service given to me while I took hours to choose the fabrics for this project.

Thank you to my students for testing the teaching techniques and to Sarah for standing in for me at the shop while I finished this book. To Clive who supported me, encouraged me and brought me tea and his home-made cake when I was working into the night in my studio: I love you. To my clients, especially my celebrity clients who could have used any designer but chose me, I am honoured and extremely flattered. You allowed me to push my boundaries so that I could learn as I went along, and it has been a privilege dressing you. Last, but not at all least, thank you to all my readers for buying this book. Much love, as always, and happy sewing – Simon.

Suppliers

Fabrics

WWW.MACCULLOCH-WALLIS.CO.UK
For beautiful, top-end fabrics as well as millinery supplies and tools. Expect to pay top-end prices, but it's well worth it.

WWW.CHEAPFABRICS.CO.UK
Good quality fabrics at very reasonable prices. This is an excellent site for silks and calico.

WWW.WHALEYS-BRADFORD.LTD.UK/
RANGE_FABRICS.HTM
Top quality wool crêpe. Available in black and navy or undyed.

WWW.ABAKHAN-ONLINESHOP.CO.UK/
ACATALOG/DRESS.HTML
Always lots of clearance lines; keep visiting the site for the best deals.

WWW.CANDH.CO.UK/
A good, all-round selection of fabrics at very keen prices.

Pattern-making supplies

WWW.MORPLAN.CO.UK
An excellent store for design equipment and consumables.

WWW.SHOBENFASHIONMEDIA.COM/
For patterns, books and designer set squares.

Machines

WWW.HOME-SEWING.COM/ENG/
INDEX.PHP
For Toyota sewing and overlock machines.

WWW.BROTHERMACHINES.COM

WWW.JANOME.CO.UK

WWW.HUSQVARNAVIKING.COM

WWW.PFAFF.COM

WWW.BERNINA.COM

Index

A

attaching crystals 95
attaching sequins 94

B

bagged-in hems 36
ball gown, planning 11
basques 75
beaded lace 90
beads 94
Belle dress 156–71
    embellishing 169–70
    variation 171
bias binding 38
bias cutting 68
bias-bagged hems 38–9
bias-bound hems 40
big hoop sequins 94
blocks
    body block 54–67
    fitting 73
    full block 68–73
body blocks 54–67
boned bodices 75–81
boned seams 41–2
boning 41
bottom-heavy figure 86, 88
bows 133–4
brocade 92
buttons and rouleau loops
    47–50

C

calico 19
charmeuse 90, 92
chiffon 93, 96
column figure 86, 87
corsages 96, 99
crepe 90, 92
crepe de chine 90
cross cutting 68
crystals 95
curved seams 24–7

D

darts 28–32
    multiple-dart run 31–2
    single-run 29–30
designer's squares 19
designs
    Belle dress 156–71
    Elegance dress 136–55
    and figure types 89
    Midnight dress 100–15
    Vintage dress 118–35
dress stands 17
drops 94
duchess satin 90
dupion 90

E

Elegance dress 136–55
    paper pattern 140–3
    making the dress 144–54
    variation 155
embellishments 94–5
    fabric flowers 96–9

embroidery 95
equipment 16–19
eyelet tape 51
eyelets 51

F

fabric flowers 96–9
fabric snips 19
fabrics 19
    for basques 75
    choosing 90–3
    embellished 95
    grain 68
    quantity needed 93
    right side 39
see also individual types
fastenings 43–51
    buttons and rouleau
    loops 47–50
    lacing 51
    zips 43–6
figure types 86–9
    and making your own
    design 89
fitting 89
fitting body block 73
foundation garments 73, 89
French seams 34–5
full blocks 68–73

G

georgette 93

To request a full catalogue of GMC titles, please contact:

GMC Publications Ltd, Castle Place, 166 High Street,
Lewes, East Sussex, BN7 1XU, United Kingdom

Tel: 01273 488005 Fax: 01273 402866 www.gmcbooks.com